The
IMMORTALS

Derek & Julia Parker

The IMMORTALS

McGRAW-HILL BOOK COMPANY
New York · St Louis · San Francisco · Dusseldorf · Mexico · Toronto

Endpapers: Fairy Feller's Master-stroke. Painting by Richard Dadd (1819–87)
Pages 1 and 7: Elf on an insect. Painting by Richard Doyle (1824–83)
Title page: Oberon Titania and Puck with Fairies dancing. Painting by William Blake (1757–1827)

A Webb&Bower Book
Edited, designed and produced by
Webb & Bower Ltd., Exeter, England

Designed by Jacqueline Small

Picture Research by Anne-Marie Ehrlich

Library of Congress Cataloging in Publication Data
Parker, Derek.
   The immortals.

   Bibliography: p.
   Includes index.
   1. Mythology.   2. Folk-lore.   I. Parker,
Julia.   II. Title.
BL311.P37   291.2'11   76–6940
   ISBN 0–07–048493–7

PRINTED IN ENGLAND

Contents

Introduction

'A man has only one way of being immortal on this earth,' wrote Jean Giraudoux, the French novelist and dramatist; 'he has to forget he is mortal.' Immortality was one of the wishful gifts – like bravery, good looks, success with women – bestowed on their favourite gods by the men and women who built the various great structures of world mythology. Others received less attractive characteristics: obesity, ugliness, meanness, unrequited lust. Since life in the various pantheons had to mirror life on earth – for what was myth except an attempt to create models for living and doing? – the gods occasionally died; but for the most part only to be resurrected like Osiris or Christ, or reincarnated like Vishnu, or to live on in some other dimension even more remote than the supernatural one into which they had been born.

Mythology can tell us much about the character of primitive man – illustrating, for instance, his very considerable and inventive intelligence. The complexity of the mythology of Olympus or Asgard was as great as that of the modern 'mythological' states of Nazi Germany or Soviet Russia: the characters of Set or Loki as complex as those of Stalin or Hitler. Myth teaches us to regard our ancestors with considerable respect, both for their imagination and their intellectual achievement.

As David Hume, the eighteenth-century philosopher, put it: 'The first idea of religion arose not from a contemplation of the works of nature, but from a concern with regard to the events of life.' Myth is *personal* – it represents man's earliest attempts to illustrate his own life in the universe in which he found himself so surprisingly stranded. Faced with the great inexplicable mysteries – birth, love, death – and

with his own impulses to war, theft, lust and murder, he sought at least to make them familiar by inventing gods who shared them. Of course he explained nothing by this: we are no nearer determining what precisely happens at the moment of death, or when that moment occurs for that matter, than the Egyptians were when they invented the story of Hathor, the good cow, hiding in the foliage of a sycamore-tree to welcome the dead with bread and water. And at least the myth had the virtues of poetry and imagination.

Psychologists attempt to explain the forces which prompt an individual to sadism or the lust for power; but they may approach no nearer the centre of the mystery than the anonymous story-tellers who 'explained' the horrors of everyday life by inventing stories of the bloody adventures of their gods.

Is myth now dead to us, except as a set of marvellous anecdotes? The most recent great myth might seem to be the Christian one, which itself bears echoes of equally powerful earlier stories: the memory of the whole world weeping for the death of Balder, or of Odin hanging in a tree, wounded by a spear. It is not too much to suggest that in a thousand years the history of Christ too may seem as much a 'story' as the tales of Balder and Odin. Osiris reigned, after all, for over three thousand years, worshipped for a longer period than any known divinity, and now his cult is dead.

The myths of contemporary life thrive in the comic strip or in science fiction – in Superman or even Desperate Dan, and in SF television serials on both sides of the Atlantic. Overtly, these heroes may not have the same purpose as

Adonis or Bes or Loki; but they are as invincible, their predicaments reflecting our own. Then there are the modern political myths: the myths of totalitarian states to left and right, of the all-conquering Aryan of Nazi Germany or the invincible Common Man of Russia – and the heavens and hells described by their inventors. The promises made by Hitler or Stalin of lands of milk, honey and perpetual justice are as unreal as the tales of Olympus or indeed heaven.

All that can be done in a brief introduction to mythology is to sketch in outlines. We have chosen to concentrate on the *characters* of myth rather than on explicatory myths of life or death. And what personalities there are: Zeus himself, so all-conquering as to become almost a bore, and yet so constantly innovatory in his amorous escapades, so ingenious in disguise, so inventive in adventure; the Bannik or wash-house god of the Slavs; Bes the enthusiastic god of women's toiletries; Ch'ang-O, who stole the cup of immortality from her husband; Njörd, the bisexual god whose beautiful feet obtained him the love of a giant's daughter. . . . They all have remarkable living presences and their complex adventures would fill (and have filled) many volumes. The reading list to be found at the end of this book should help those who wish to trace any particular god further than we have followed him. Here may be found a few of the leading characters of world myth, often – as the *Who's Who* shows – distantly or more closely related. 'You can change your faith without changing gods, and vice versa', as Stanislaus Lec reminded us. Only the gods' names sometimes distinguish them, for the immortals of different cultures often reflect the same characteristics, of the black-and-white hero, villain, lover – archetypes of man.

Such a rudimentary account can only whet the appetite. It is a very personal look at the subject, and our tone has been determinedly light-hearted. Like man, the gods he created in his own image have his faults, take up his own ridiculous postures, adopt his own sad, comic attitudes of bravery or cowardice, love, lust or grief. We must laugh at them for fear we may find ourselves weeping for ourselves. Anyone who, still retaining some respect for Osiris or indeed still worshipping Krishna, most sympathetic of immortals, might remember the words of G.K. Chesterton: 'It is the test of a good religion whether you can make a joke about it.'

Myth not only reveals the theology and psychology of primitive man, but has much to say about the nature of man's personality. Perhaps no story which has retained its force, been told again and again by the story-tellers and writers of many generations, can fail to do this. *Hamlet* reveals us to ourselves through the agency of one genius; the myths of Greece through the agency of man's own psyche, reflected in many mirrors and focused by the final theme and thrust of the narrative. We hope these sketches will encourage the reader to delve deeper.

Readers using the Index or *Who's Who* should make allowances for the fact that the names of the gods of various cultures are often differently spelled or transliterated by different scholars and writers. We have always attempted to use the most familiar spelling, and hope that any confusion will not cause too much irritation.

Derek and Julia Parker

Spirits of Earth

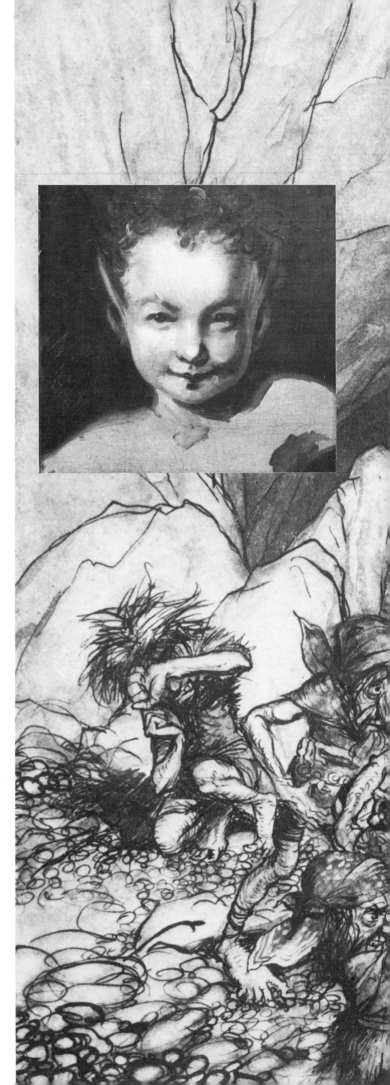

It was the Sicilian philosopher Empedocles, in the middle of the fifth century BC, who first put forward the theory that earth, air, fire and water are the four elements from which everything in the universe is made, though these elements had of course been instinctively known to man as soon as he was a conscious being. Not surprisingly, the earliest myths were rooted in the earth which bore him up, the water which quenched his thirst and cleansed him, the fire which brought light to darkness, cooked his food and warmed him, and the winds which buffeted the sea and hills and howled mysteriously through the trees.

From the deepest past come the many names of the earth-mother – Ga-Tum-Dug or Bau, Innini or Gula, or Ninkhursag. The earth as a receiver of seed was naturally female – she accepted the bodies of the dead, too, in another form of 'planting', which became a solemn ceremony in the myths of North America, West Africa and Mongolia. In North American Indian legend, earth is the Mother of all, and the sky the Father, while in an Egyptian papyrus of 1000 BC the sky-goddess Nut stretches herself in a great arc over her recumbent but obviously potent brother, Geb, the earth-god. The Algonquin Indians call earth Nokomis, or Grandmother, who at her ample breasts suckles plants, animals and men; for the ancient Peruvians, she was Pachamamma.

The Greeks called her Gaea, who appeared out of the Stygian blackness of Chaos and gave birth to Uranus, the sky with its stars, and then to the high mountains and the sea with its ever-moving waves. Finally, after an incestuous mating with Uranus, she bore the first race of men – the Titans. Unlike many of the earth-goddesses, she had a personality which was uniquely important, since it was from her that the whole of creation sprang, as man – or at least the primitive Greeks – knew it. She was the supreme goddess worshipped not only by humans but by the other gods, for she had created both the immortal and mortal races. Later, her cult merged into that of Rhea, who is said to have originated in Crete and whom the Greeks identified with Cybele, the goddess of caves, who was worshipped on the tops of mountains and commanded the wild beasts that flocked to guard her.

Men also had their part to play in the personifications of earth. (So, indeed, had animals: the Kato Indians of California, for instance, believed that earth was a vast horned animal

floundering through primeval waters, and steered by Nagaicho, creator of the tribe.) In ancient Egypt it was Geb, the earth-god, who would lie face downward while vegetation sprouted from his back. Separated from his wife (who in the true Egyptian tradition was also his sister), he constantly wept for her, the undulations of his heaving body representing the hills and valleys of the landscape.

But in mythology the earth has mainly been female, sometimes simply in gender, rather than as a personalized woman. The Russians worshipped the earth as Mati-Syra-Zemlya, or 'Moist Mother Earth', yet they believed her divinity was explicit and that she need not appear in human form. A peasant would dig a small hole and put his ear to the earth, hoping to hear her voice; he would pour oil into the earth, which drank it greedily, and place a lump of earth on his head when taking a specially important oath.

The establishment of commanding earth-gods and -goddesses did not preclude the existence of other immortal beings of an earthly nature – generally they were rather lumpish and unpleasant, or simply of a cloddish mischievousness. It is these who live on in folk tradition, regarded as living beings until comparatively recently. Pan is one who springs to mind. He was earthy by nature, having been born with the legs, horns and beard of a goat, as the result of an unfortunate liaison between his mother Penelope and his father Hermes, who had for some reason best known to himself approached her disguised as a goat. Pan lives in grottoes, and is especially protective of herds of goats and sheep. His goatish disposition has brought him an indifferent reputation, and indeed various nymphs (including Syrinx, who had to be changed into a reed to escape him, and even then he cut her and made her into a pan-pipe) can testify to his incorrigible sexual appetite. For some time he lived exclusively in Arcadia, in the central Peloponnese, where his cult was born. Then he travelled to Attica, and eventually achieved a sanctuary on the Acropolis itself. Though the story was put about that he died at the moment of the birth of Christ, he seems to have survived in various forms and in various countries. The family resemblance to Aristaeus, for instance, is too strong not to suppose that that deity, with his predilection for nectar and ambrosia, is Pan in light disguise. In Boeotia he married the beautiful Autonoë, and sired Actaeon; in Thrace, it was he who fell in love with Eurydice, and caused

her death. Soon afterwards, with excellent timing, he vanished spectacularly from the top of Mount Haemus, only to reappear as Priapus in Asia Minor, with a phallus of such immense proportions and indefatigable industry that the flocks of animals of the mountains and plains reproduced themselves prolifically in imitative admiration.

Puck, the peculiarly British earth-spirit, is a decided if distant relation of Pan's. He is a much less insistently amorous immortal, confining his mischievousness to the home, doing housework in exchange for cream or cake. According to a biography of him written in 1588, he is the child of a young girl and a 'hee-fayrie', and one of his attributes is to be able to change himself into any animal at will: travellers tempted to mount a strange horse on a wild moor have occasionally found themselves left in the middle of a stream with nothing but a saddle between their legs. Unlike his colleagues the fairies, Puck is a coarse being (even his other names – Gruagach, Urisk, Boggart, Dobie, Hob – suggest an earthy quality), and he figures often in extremely *risqué* anecdotes. Maureen Duffy, in *The Erotic World of Faery*, has pointed out how strongly he resembles the phallus – not least because, naturally naked, he tends to become

ineffective if anyone attempts to clothe him. His sexuality relates him to Pan as surely as to the Lar, a short, squat figure with curly hair who was invoked in Rome at the time of a marriage.

Dwarfs and giants are less pleasant beings than Pan or Puck. The most famous dwarfs can be found in Teutonic mythology, and should be distinguished from elves, who can sometimes be as large as men and twice as handsome. Dwarfs have faces like men (ugly men, with wrinkled, leathery skins), but are generally either flat-footed, duck-footed, or have feet pointing backwards. The habit of dressing them, as in the unkind sculptures sold as garden ornaments, in green suits and little pointed red hats, is accurate: that seems to be their invariable wear. They are of the earth, earthy, living in the darkest of caverns and venturing forth only with the cloaks by which they can make themselves invisible, and often disguised as toads. Miners often come across them, and sometimes establish reasonably close relations with them. In Cornwall, for instance, the buccas (the local dwarfish name) are not averse from helping with the work, though their thieving habits made it necessary to invent the Cornish pasty (that unique and delicious dish consisting of meat, potato and onion, wrapped in pastry and baked) and sign it with a cross to protect human food from their greed. The tin-miners of Cornwall were always delighted to hear a bucca busily mining away, for all dwarfs have an infallible nose for precious metals, which of course led them into all the fuss and bother of the thirteenth-century German poem, the *Nibelungenlied*, as a result of their guardianship of the rich treasure stolen from them and their chief, Alberich, by the fascist bully-boy Siegfried.

Among other things, dwarfs are rightly valued for their skill as blacksmiths and jewellers: they made Odin his famous spear Gungnir, and Thor his hammer; for Freya they designed a magnificent necklace, and for Frey a golden boar. And in their spare time they are excellent bakers. Ironically, despite their odd feet, they are particularly fond of dancing. They can also see into the future, and consequently are excellent meteorologists. They can be free with presents to people they like, and a dwarfish gift is likely to turn to gold in the hand. But on the whole they are a snappish lot, except perhaps the kobolds of Germany, who often live in the cellars of farm-houses and are extremely good farm-workers, with the additional bonus of bringing good luck.

The 'Long Man' whose outline is carved into the chalky hillside near Wilmington in Sussex. Like other similar figures, this may date from the late Iron Age, and was probably 'drawn' by the inhabitants of one of the many hill forts in the area. The Long Man may have been a chief, but has been given godlike stature (though emasculated, over the ages)

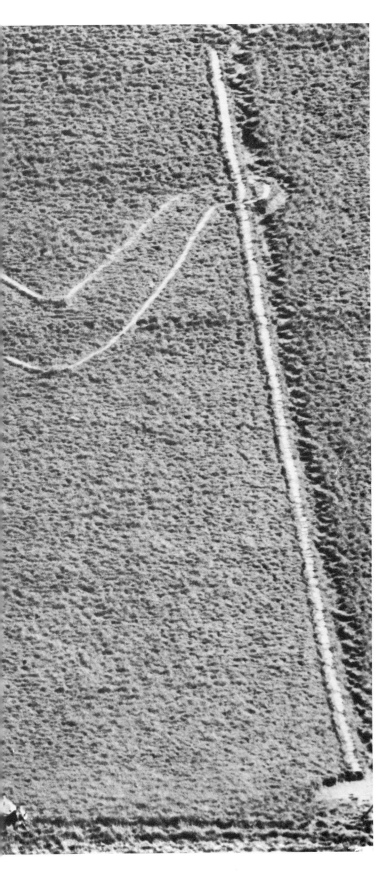

While the Teutonic dwarfs are by far the best known, it should not be imagined that dwarfs are invariably of middle Europe: the Egyptians had a dwarf-god, Bes – a bald-headed, bearded specimen of unpleasant aspect dressed in a leopard-skin, whose fondness for music (he played the tambourine and harp) and dancing betrayed his kinship with his Teutonic brothers. Under the New Kingdom he was perhaps the most popular of all the Egyptian gods, a conscientious protector of sheep; but later (surprisingly, considering his appearance) he became a special guardian of expectant mothers and an expert in make-up. Moses is said to have exterminated him, yet his image is still to be found (at Karnak, for example), and is strongly suspected of leaving its pillar during the night so that he can go about his ancient duties. Even as far from Europe as Mexico, there is a band of relatively unknown dwarfs, the Tepictoton, whose ill-nature required the sacrifice of children to placate them. The North American Indians and Eskimos also have their dwarf myths.

The Seven Dwarfs of Snow White, made so famous by Walt Disney (though in a form any self-respecting dwarf would rigorously reject), originated with Jacob and Wilhelm Grimm: but the story has been found in a similar form in Asia Minor, in Ireland and in North and West Africa. In all the variations, the dwarfs are busily mining for gold – a tradition from the earliest times.

If dwarfs (pace Happy, Grumpy, Sneezy and the rest), are generally speaking rather unpleasant, giants are doubly so: naturally, for it seems most probable that they originated not in some race of extra-large humans, or even in the occasional seven-feet tall man, but as personifications of violent winds or cyclones, earthquakes or eruptions. Giants have some claim to be the oldest immortals of all, predating even the gods as the original denizens of earth. The giants of Greek mythology were the least beguiling of creatures – not only immense in size, but with serpents' legs and feet formed of the heads of reptiles. They were born in full armour, carrying spears, and in launching an attack on Olympus they shifted whole mountains to build ramps to their objective. The gods managed to defeat them, though they still occasionally stir. When the giant Enceladus moves in his grave beneath Sicily, the whole island quakes.

Eskimo and North American Indian folklore is rich in giant stories. In the Eastern Woodlands, 15

Prometheus, making a man of earth, attaches his left arm. From an early illustration of Ovid's *Metamorphosis* (c 1531)

Right: God transforms chaos into life. From an illustrated edition of Ovid's *Metamorphosis* (c 1531)

Tryggvason forced one of them to build a church – since when they have gone to ground.

The most famous English giant was the one disposed of by Jack – or maybe by King Arthur, who, in Sir Thomas Malory's *Morte Darthur* and earlier in Geoffrey of Monmouth's *Historia Regum Britanniae*, fought the prototype, whose home was in the castle on St Michael's Mount, a rock off Penzance, Cornwall, and who, looking out from his vantage-point, rejoiced with this well-known cry:

> *Fee, fi, fo fum,*
> *I smell the blood of an Englishman!*

Jack, who indeed was English rather than Cornish, remains the only European hero to triumph over a giant by natural wit and dexterity rather than by force of arms. He was said by Sir Francis Palgrave to have landed 'from the very keels and warships which conveyed Hengist and Horsa, and Ebba the Saxon'. Ever afterwards he was recognized by the engraving on his sword:

> *Here's the right valiant Cornishman*
> *Who slew the Giant Cormilan . . .*

indicating the honorary freedom of the county conferred upon him by the Mayor and Corporation of Penzance.

There are many other carefully recorded giants in English history. Some were mortal, like John Middleton, a man of nine feet three inches from Hale in Lancashire who, attacked by a bull in 1620, simply threw it over a neighbouring hedge. Geoffrey of Monmouth believed Britain was originally inhabited by a race of giants, the last two being Gog and Magog, whose statues stand in the Guildhall in the City of London. Perhaps it is this lost race which is commemorated by the figures carved in the chalk soil of hills all over Britain. The most famous of these is the Cerne Abbas giant, over 180 feet high, and carved on the side of a Dorset hill, his towering phallus representing abundant virility, and his lengthy club his prowess in war.

The immortals born of the element of earth – heavy as the giants, lumpish as the dwarfs – seem in a way to represent those parts of us which are chained to reality, and grumpy because of it. The ethereal, free quality of those who soar into the air, the most delightful of the elements, is enviable indeed.

Shawnee legend has it that there lives a giantess with four immense 'Boys' who can smell human blood a long way off, and indeed the giants' sense of smell is one of their most delicate attributes. It is common to the giants of Teutonic myth, and helps the giants of Scandinavia to make life a misery for humans and gods alike. Any ordinary mortal living in Scandinavia may see plenty of evidence of the ways of giants, even if they never set eyes on one. Booming voices are heard among the hills when thunder rolls, and storm-clouds racing across the sky are put in a flurry by some giant scudding after a pretty girl he hopes to capture.

The *Nibelungenlied* tells of twelve giants who live in the mountains: their grumbling can be heard from the depths of chasms, and they still cause avalanches and floods. Though giants in other parts of the world vanished soon after the spread of Christianity, they were still active in Germany as late as the thirteenth century, when Olaf

Spirits of the Air

Air is such an incorporeal substance that immortals have rarely taken charge of it. There was a god of air called Shu in ancient Egypt, and from the Campius Martius in Rome there is a bas-relief (*c.* 11 BC) actually showing Air seated on a swan next to the earth-goddess Tellus Mater. However, air has been the element for many immortals – from angels to fairies, from the Valkyries to Boreas.

Air in movement – the turbulent wind – has had its gods from the very earliest times. In Babylonia and Assyria, Adad, standing on a bull with thunderbolts in each hand, ruled the storm, roaring in thunder through the black clouds. In his benevolent moods, fortunately rather more frequent than his rages, he also controlled the gentle zephyrs which bring the rains and encourage crops to grow. In early Phoenician mythology, the air presided over the growth of all things. The light winds of summer were actually called *Desire*, and were believed to

have created all nature – Aer and Aura, air and breath, represented the spirits of intelligence and of humanity, and from their union came the cosmic egg itself.

The Greeks had four divinities to rule the four winds: the sons of the dawn and the sky – Boreas, the north wind, Zephyrus, the west wind, Eurus the east wind, and Notus, the south wind. Boreas was a somewhat licentious immortal (not an uncommon phenomenon, admittedly), carrying off the beautiful Oreithyia, changing himself into a stallion and fathering on the mares of Erichthonius the famous brood of horses so light that they could run over a field of standing corn without bruising a single ear of grain. Zephyrus was not the calming influence one might have hoped: at first, at least, he took particular pleasure in raising storms at sea, later wedding a harpy and raising the two horses which drew Achilles' chariot. In middle age, he settled down to become a sweet breeze over Elysium. With

their brothers, these two live on the Aeolian Islands, ruled (as far as is possible) by Aeolus, the inventor of the sail, who once placed some contrary winds in a wine-skin as a present for the adventuring Odysseus, who unwisely opened the skin to take a look and let them escape. Aeolus was elevated to supreme god of wind in Roman mythology, and lives on the island of Lipari, off the north coast of Sicily.

Apart from the major wind-gods, there are some minor deities such as Typhon, spirit of the hurricane, and Echidna his wife, a horrific mermaid. The harpies, too, are storm-goddesses.

The gods who rule violent storms are perhaps not pure air gods: Thor, or Donner, the god of thunder in Teutonic myth, for instance, seems more akin to earth than air. The Chinese god My Lord Thunder, too, is a solid, ugly personage, with a blue body, whose wings seem more suited for decoration than for flight. He makes an infernal din by hitting the drums he carries with his hammer, and he also has a chisel with which he carves up impertinent mortals unwise enough to get in his way.

In Japan, a wind-god and -goddess preside over storm and calm weather. These two, Shina-Tsu-Hiko and Shina-To-Be, were created from the breath of the god Izanagi, both filling the space between heaven and earth and providing a sort of pneumatic support for the earth itself.

Immortals, but not goddesses, are the Valkyries, a drunken and uncontrollable lot who in Teutonic myth support warriors in battle, and are unable to restrain themselves from joining in. They decide who shall die in the fight, and are permitted to choose who of these shall be promoted to an immortality of drinking beer and mead at the feasts of Odin. Usually seen in war-helmets and with spears, they have unexpectedly graceful swan-plumage which enables them to fly. Occasionally they slip this plumage off in order to bathe, when a canny human who manages to steal it has the power to command them – a happy chance which accounts for many legends, including the original story of Brünnhilde, as told by Wagner in his *Ring* saga.

If one is forced to accept the word of fourteenth-century cabalists, it is surprising that there is room for any of these immortals, for the air is also full of angels. They counted 301,655,722 of them – Origen, one of the Fathers of the Church, pointing out that they 'multiply like flies', while St Augustine was of the opinion that 'every visible thing in this world is put under the charge of an angel'. Furthermore, the cabalists presumably only counted Christian angels, whereas there are others – seven are specifically mentioned in the Koran, for example.

Angelography is a difficult study, since so many angels appear under numerous pseudonyms – Gabriel is also Abrael, Abry-el, Jabriel, Jibril, Prevuil, Radueriel, Revan-Bakhsh, Seferiel, Sorush and Vrevoil. They also suffer sometimes from acute schizophrenia: Camael, who goes about dressed as a leopard, serves in hell as Count Palatine and ruler of the evil planet Mars, while at the same time

appearing benevolently in heaven as an archangel, and is recorded as having led a troop of twelve thousand spirits to escort God at the promulgation of the Holy Law.

The sex of angels is somewhat uncertain, though more of them appear to be male than female. There are one or two obviously female angels such as Shekinah, who lives with happily married couples, Eisheth Zenunim, the angel of prostitution, and her three friends Naamah, Mahlaht, and Lilith – the last perhaps the most famous of heaven's whores, Adam's mistress, who when coupling with Sammael, Prince of Demons, actually shook the legs of the Divine Throne (and seems to have been remarkably corporeal, for an air-immortal).

The saints and prophets have sometimes taken a rather equivocal view of angels. St Paul seems to have been far less enthusiastic about them than might have been expected, and their behaviour is certainly sometimes a little uncircumspect. They have been known to cuckold elderly husbands incapable of satisfying their wives, to strike men with hysterical dumbness or blindness and paralyse others, and to frighten the life out of innocent asses.

Apart from these somewhat substantial angels, there are the angels of visions, flying about the throne of heaven. About the mechanics of their flight we know little except that they are undoubtedly adept, for they can travel from place to place in a flash. Michael, among others, can it seems appear in three heavens simultaneously, so needs to be fairly quick on his wings.

The hierarchy of angels is also a matter of some argument. Enoch, one of the earliest authorities, placed the top seven archangels in the following order: Uriel, Raphael, Raguel, Michael, Zerachiel, Gabriel and Remiel. St Ambrose placed angels as a species fairly low in the whole heavenly hierarchy: first came Seraphim, then Cherubim, then Dominations, Thrones, Principalities, Powers, Virtues, Archangels and then at last the ordinary rank-and-file angel.

But that angels were of importance to the early Church is unarguable: the seasons, days, and the very hours of the day and night, all had their separate angels. The twelve months of the year, starting with January, had them in this sequence: Gabriel, Barchiel, Machidiel, Asmodel, Ambriel, Muriel, Verchiel, Hamaliel, Uriel, Barbiel, Adnachiel and Hanael. The same twelve ruled over the astrological signs, with Machidiel ruling Aries, and so on in the same order through the zodiac. The planets had their angelic rulers, too. Sammael looked after Mars; Raphael guards the sun, Michael, Mercury; Gabriel, the moon; Kafziel, Saturn; Zadkiel, Jupiter; and Aniel, Venus.

The connection between angels and fairies must seem somewhat tenuous, though fairies were often spoken of as rebel angels who had been thrown out of heaven but had not fallen quite as far as hell. There is certainly some resemblance between good angels and the Trooping Fairies of English legend. An angel is usually a fine figure of a spirit, and the Trooping Fairies too are among the most attractive of all immortals – humans have been struck dumb

by their beauty as they pass by through the woodland on a bright moonlit night, riding in procession on white horses hung with silver bells to splendid feasts. However, they cannot fly. The flying fairy is a much smaller, prettier creature, able to soar through the air and levitate smaller humans and capable of taking on any shape it pleases – a bee or a bird, or even a four-leaf clover. It is far from angelic, given to stealing the babies of nursing mothers and replacing them with an elf. Even now, though electric light is evidently unsympathetic to fairies, they can claim attention in rural parts of Europe, and have even been surprised by the camera.

Perhaps the most enchanting of individual fairies is the inimitable Ariel, Shakespeare's creation in *The Tempest*, as natural a being of the air as Caliban, in the same play, is of the earth. Coleridge described him:

In air he lives, from air he derives his being, in air he acts; and all his colours and properties seem to have been obtained from the rainbow and the skies.

But he can take on the properties of fire, too, as when Prospero sends him to strike terror into the crew of Alonzo's ship:

> *now on the beak,*
> *Now in the waist, the deck, in every cabin,*
> *I flamed amazement; sometimes I'd divide*
> *And burn in many places; on the top-mast,*
> *The yards and bowsprit would I flame*
> * distinctly,*
> *Then meet, and join . . .*

He would obviously have been at home with the fire-spirits, too.

Spirits of Fire

The main way of obtaining fire in many early civilizations was by rubbing sticks together, so it is hardly surprising that in myths of South America, Australia, Africa, Asia and Europe, fire was associated with trees, or with *a* tree, in which it was usually hidden by the mortal who had stolen it from the gods. In Polynesia, a Maori myth tells how Maui begged fire from his grandmother Mahuika, who produced it in such superabundance from her fingers and toes that it set light to the trees around her, which ever afterwards have produced it for any man who has caressed their wood with sufficient ardour. The Tembe of Brazil also turn to trees for fire, but believe that it was hidden in their branches by an old man who stole it from the vultures which originally guarded it. Some North American Indians believe that fire was originally stolen by animals, who passed it one to another so quickly that its owner never could recover it.

The natural connection between fire and the heat of the sun led men to assume that one sprang from

the other, though there were other theories. The Wagawaga of New Guinea believe that an old woman was fire's rightful owner, and that she kept it in her vagina, producing it as and when it was needed, while American Indian tribes personalized fire itself as 'Our Grandfather', whose smoke carried their prayers up to God.

In Europe, however, fire naturally belonged to Zeus, originally the god of the sky, but later the supreme, omnipotent god. Prometheus stole it from him in a stalk of fennel, and as a result was bound to a rock on Mount Caucasus where an immortal eagle feeds for ever on his immortal liver. Prometheus had taken fire from the forge of Hephaestus, the cripple later thrown from Olympus by Zeus to set up a smithy in or near the volcano on the island of Lemnos, from which later he moved west to Attica and Sicily. Olympus was the poorer, for there he

had forged many beautiful things including Zeus' throne, Helios' winged chariot and Hercules' cuirass.

There has usually been a distinction of some sort between celestial, sacred fire, and the fire of the domestic hearth – of which, in Greece, Hestia was goddess, with her special temple at Delphi, the centre of the universe. Kamado-No-Kami is god of the Japanese kitchen-range, while there are two other gods for non-culinary fires. Tsao-wang, in China, is not only a hearth-god, but keeps a strict record of a family's behaviour, for later reference after death.

Fire itself was personalized in a number of gods: Atar, in ancient Persia, Xiuhetcuhtli with the Aztecs, Agni with the Hindus, and in Japan Kagu-Zuchi, a particularly irascible god, from whom the Japanese had difficulty in protecting their wooden houses. There were many subsidiary gods of the sun, of lightning, volcanoes, and the underworld or hell, with which fire is often associated. In Emma-Hoo, the Japanese hell, there are eight regions of fire and eight of ice; in the Chinese hell, the guardians are the Shih-tien Yen-wang, who make considerable use of fire. For sheer fiery sadism, however, the Christian hell takes a lot of beating – which is why Satan and his devils represent fire for the European world to a greater extent than any pagan god. The Christian hell has always been fiery; as Milton typically described it:

> A dungeon horrible, on all sides round,
> As one great furnace, flamed; yet from those flames
> No light; but rather darkness visible
> Served only to discover sights of woe,
> Regions of sorrow, doleful shades
> . . . torture without end
> Still urges, and a fiery deluge, fed
> With ever-burning sulphur unconsumed.

The Devil himself (who has a chapter of his own) presides over hell as general manager, and is naturally assisted by smaller devils in great number. It has sometimes been assumed that every wicked man after death becomes a devil, and therefore it is hardly surprising that hell is well populated with torturers (but who is there, then, to torture?). The Talmud suggests that at the last count there were 7,405,926 devils in hell; Feyerabend's *Theatrum Diabolorum*, a book published by followers of Martin Luther, put the number at

23

Early illustrated manuscripts convey vividly the superstitious horror their authors and illustrators felt when they thought of hell.
Right: The mouth of hell, from an early manuscript, with devils and horrid animals herding the damned downward

2,665,866,746,664; while others hold that one-tenth of the angels of God who took part in Lucifer's rebellion became devils. There seems to be no accurate or dependable set of statistics available, nor any prospect of a properly ordered census.

Theology, indeed, is somewhat vague about devils altogether. There seems to be a hierarchy of them, but though St Thomas speaks of it, he does not set it out; nor does anyone else. It is uncertain, too, as to what extent devils have power over human beings. Though they are certainly not as intelligent as angels, no one is decided on how much more intelligent they are than men. Is it true, as Honorius Augustodunensis suggested, that they know all about man's evil thoughts but cannot divine his good ones? Is it the case, as Origen supposed, that they are excellent astrologers, able to discover the future from the movements of the planets? After all, Lactantius believed astrology to have been invented by the Devil.

Whatever their nature, their imperviousness to fire is without doubt, and they do not even need protective clothing, unlike one Emperor of India, who wore a suit made of a thousand salamander skins (the salamander has the rare attribute of being so cold that it can dance happily in the flames of the hottest fire). They are naturally immune to the flames which St John of Damascus kindly supposed to be figurative, but which most Christian authorities believed to be actual. St Augustine was of the opinion that if all the waters of the earth flowed into hell, their effect on its fires would be unnoticeable.

Various witnesses actually descended into hell, and brought back eye-witness reports for the benefit of the sinning majority. Alberico and Wettin and Tundal, three monks, all left descriptions, and fire was all-pervading. In it, devils, quarrelsome and given to beating one another up from time to time, capered happily unscathed.

There is perhaps a distinction to be made between Christian devils (or devils involved in fighting Christian ideals) and demons, more usually associated with other religions. The demons of Indian mythology, for instance, are of a different character – often almost indistinguishable from the gods themselves. The Indian term for demon is *asura*, and *asuras* and *devas* (or gods) are both descended from Prajapati, the master of humanity. Having chosen falsehood rather than truth, *asuras*

24

have naturally prospered, and even now can sometimes triumph over the gods.

The Japanese recognize eighteen generals and eighty thousand demons under the direct orders of Emma-Hoo, while the earth is roamed by a number of Oni whose job it is to catch sinners and take them in a fiery chariot to hell. (It may be that they are less successful than the criteria suggest, for they appear with red or green bodies and the heads of oxen or horses, so must be fairly recognizable.) In Scandinavia, the *fylgja* is a sort of *alter ego* who, unlike the immaterial Christian soul, can become a material demon, pagan and evil. To all these evil spirits, fire seems a natural and welcome element.

Tundal saw, in his vision of hell, a vast monster also happily squatting in the flames, large as a mountain and with eyes like burning hills and a mouth large enough to contain nine thousand armed men. A dragon? Well, in the Middle Ages the dragon had come to symbolize the Devil, and the bright flames and smoke which issued from his nostrils emphasized his combustible nature.

The dragon population is strictly limited, for the female has the disconcerting habit of biting off her mate's head while making love, and the baby dragon, not content to wait for a more conventional birth, eats its way out of its mother's womb, thus destroying her also. Born with a fiery belly, dragons are inherently thirsty beasts, particularly fond of elephants' blood, which they believe to have a cooling effect. They have affinities with both water and air: certainly they can fly. Bartholomew Anglicus used to see them, in flocks of four or five, tails tied together, soaring over the face of Germany, near Magdeburg. They are given to urinating while in flight, and 'dragons' water' is extremely dangerous, tending to burn off any limb on which it falls.

The Phoenix, a much pleasanter flying creature, appears in Egyptian and Grecian myth, and its activities were reported until relatively recently. Originally a symbol of the sun, it is a lonely and singular bird with a long life-span (perhaps as long as twelve thousand years). It was commonly believed that when the end of that life was reached, the bird built itself a nest of spices which the sun ignited: the Phoenix then fanned the flames with its wings, and cremated itself. A new bird arose from a tiny worm emerging from the ashes – fire used, not for the first time, as a symbol of regeneration.

25

Spirits of Water

The Assyrians and Babylonians believed that water was the original element from which the world arose, and Enki, its god, was assisted by his daughter Nanshe, who cared for springs and canals. The rivers themselves, so important for irrigation, also became gods. In Egypt, Ea was the counterpart of Enki: a goat-god with a fish's tail, he was also the god of all knowledge, and one of the three great gods of Egypt.

Greece had its freshwater gods, too – among them Achelous and Asopus, Cephissus and Alpheius – and the sea was very important to the Greeks, Poseidon, an earlier god than Zeus and as powerful, ruling over it. Living in a magnificent palace, glittering with gold, beneath the surface of the Aegean, he rises from it in a chariot drawn by splendid horses shod with bronze, to surf over the bright waves surrounded by playful sea-monsters. He has a vast retinue of mistresses and innumerable progeny. His time thus fully occupied, he has various deputies who help to rule the waves – one of them Old Father Neptune, now invoked by Western travellers crossing the equator, yet a very minor god indeed, originally only appealed to in cases of drought.

Nereus, the 'Old Man of the Sea', is helpful to sailors; Phorcys is his opposite, a malignant storm-raiser; Glaucus forecasts these storms; Proteus looks after seals. Then there are the Sirens and Tritons. The original Triton was a half-man, half-fish, a benevolent god. Sirens are malevolent creatures with irresistible voices, originally able to fly, but now grounded, their wings removed after they were vanquished in a song-contest with the Muses. They used to sit on the coast of southern Italy, tempting sailors to their deaths, until Orpheus in turn charmed them and they were changed into rocks, which they remain.

Northern races have perhaps less picturesque water-gods. The Finns have Ahto, who with his wife Vellamo lives in black slime in the heart of a rock-face. He has unattractive henchmen like Vizi-ember, a Magyar god who lives in rivers and lakes and demands human sacrifice. More attractive are the water-babies of the American Indians – small, mischievous creatures, sometimes 'little men' who pull on the lines of fishermen.

Fishermen in deeper waters may find themselves up against something much more formidable than a water-baby: a mermaid, perhaps? If Ea was the first merman, the idea of beings with human torsos and

fishes' tails soon spread, and in the Middle Ages the Church encouraged it by including them in bestiaries and carving them in churches and cathedrals. A fine early eye-witness description of a mermaid occurs in Bartholomew Anglicus' *De Proprietatibus Rerum* (*c.* 1240):

Physiologus saith it is a beast of the sea wonderfully shapen as a maid from the navel upward and a fish from the navel downward, and this wonderful beast is glad and merry in tempest and sad and heavy in fair weather. With sweetness of song this beast maketh shipmen to sleep, and when she seeth that they are asleep, she goeth into the ship, and ravisheth which she may take with her, and bringeth him into a dry place, and maketh him first lie by her, and if he will not or may not, then she slayeth him and eateth his flesh.

The English westcountry has been particularly fruitful in sightings of mermaids – at Mermaid's Rock, near Lamorna, at Doom Bar, off Padstow Harbour in Cornwall (where a local fisherman took a pot-shot at a mermaid who rewarded him by choking the harbour with sand), and of course at Zennor, where there is a portrait of a local mermaid carved on a bench-end in the church.

A merman was actually caught at Orford, in Suffolk, in the twelfth century, 'having the appearance of a man in all his parts', but despite lacking the usual fish's tail he declined to remain on land and was last seen swimming sturdily out to sea. The last authentic sighting of a mermaid was as recently as 1947, when an islander of Muck, off the north-west coast of Scotland, saw one sitting on a rock combing her hair (a traditional occupation).

Nastier water-beasts lie in wait for sailors and fishermen. Bishop Erik Pontoppidan first published in the eighteenth century an account of the Kraken, an enormous sea-monster of over a mile and a half in circumference, round, flat and with many arms, which would frequently be mistaken for a small island while basking on the surface of the sea off the coast of Norway, and which when it submerged provoked a major whirlpool. It has not been seen very recently, so it may be that as Tennyson suggests

Below the thunders of the upper deep,
Far, far beneath in the abysmal sea,
His ancient, dreamless, uninvaded sleep
The Kraken sleepeth

until the last trump, when

once by man and angels to be seen
In roaring he shall rise and on the surface die.

In his lengthy and probably definitive book *The Great Sea-Serpent* (1892), the Dutch zoologist and botanist A. C. Oudemans listed 162 detailed accounts of sightings of sea-serpents between 1522 (by Olaus Magnus – a serpent fifty cubits long seen near the island of Moos, off Norway) and 1890 (by a British sea captain, David Tuits, off Long Island – 'the tail, which was coloured brown with black spots, was about 40 feet out of the water'). Dr Oudemans reached the conclusion that some sea-serpents certainly existed, issued instructions for noting down their measurements and characteristics, once caught, and discounted the excuses of disbelievers – that the sightings were really of rows of porpoises, seaweed, floating dead trees or bamboos, or whales. The existence of the Loch Ness Monster, and of many similar monsters in inland waters and bogs (especially in Ireland) has been much discussed, especially in F. W. Holiday's *The Dragon and the Disc* (London, 1973). Holiday connects them with the dragons of antiquity, and specifically with the Great Worm of Hell, reported in medieval times to be Satan's emissary on earth.

A tenth-century Irish author described this immortal monster:

Repulsive, outlandish, fierce and very
terrifying was the beast. . . .
Its front end was like a horse, with a glowing,
blazing eye in its head, sharp, bitter, furious,
angry, keen, crimson, bloody, very harsh,
rapidly rolling. Anyone would think that its
eye would go through him, as it looked at him.
It had two hideous thick legs under it in front.
Iron claws on it which struck showers of fire
from the stony rocks where they trod across
them. It had a fiery breath which burned like
embers. It had a belly like a pair of bellows.
Now the sea would boil with the extent of its
heat and its venomousness when it rushed into it.

Loch Morar on the west coast of Scotland, the deepest lake in the British Isles, was the spot on which the Great Worm was last encountered (Holiday claims) by two long-distance truck-drivers who did not stay to observe it closely.

Long, lonely hours at sea may of course prompt

29

An artist's impression of a sighting of *The Flying Dutchman* (after Hermann Hendrich, *c* 1900).
Below, left: Coleridge's Ancient Mariner sights the phantom ship: 'Are those her ribs through which the Sun/ Did peer, as through a grate? . . .' (Noel Paton, 1863)
Bottom, right: The Good Hermit, in Coleridge's poem, approaches the dreadful ghost ship in which the Ancient Mariner has taken his fearful voyage. (Noel Paton, 1863)

tales of mermaids and mermen, monsters and apparitions, and the seven seas are certainly full of the latter, some more thoroughly authenticated than others. At 4 a.m. on 11 July 1881, for instance, HRH Prince George (later King George V of England), a young cadet on board HMS *Inconstant*, entered in the ship's log a sighting of the famous ghost-ship *The Flying Dutchman*.

She emitted a strange phosphorescent light as of a phantom ship all aglow, in the midst of which light the masts, spars and sails of a brig 200 yards distant stood out in sharp relief as she came up on the port bow where also the officer of the watch from the bridge saw her, as did also the quarterdeck midshipman, who was sent forward at once to the forecastle, but on arriving there no vestige nor any sign whatever of any material ship was to be seen . . . the night being calm and clear.

A storm is the more usual setting for the *Dutchman* as she battles to round Cape Horn, beating against the wind. The captain had vowed to round the Horn in a heavy storm, or be damned. He *was* damned, and joined the ranks of the immortals to sail for ever in a ship crewed by dead, dumb men. There are other phantom ships in the immortal fleet: the *Carmilhan* in the Baltic, an anonymous vessel in the Gulf of Finland, and no less than fifteen vessels off the north-west coast of the United States, always sailing against the wind, worked by no visible crew. Even the ghost of the *Titanic* has been seen; and some other recognizable vessels, such as the *Palatine*, which appears at Black Rock, Rhode Island, on the anniversary of its wreck; and the *Alice Marr* of Gloucester, Massachusetts, which almost succeeds in making harbour – but never quite. *The Courser*, a famous vessel, sails with her mast and sails towering to the clouds; they dip majestically to avoid the sun and moon.

Much more agreeable than these sea-monsters and sea-ghosts are the nymphs which haunt the springs of Greece: the Oreads, the Napaeae, the Hylaeorae and the Auloniads. The Oreads include perhaps the most famous nymph of all, Echo, whose voice is all that remains of her (her constant chatter disturbed her mistress, Hera). The delicious and ever-young beauty of the nymphs has its counterpart at sea, in the Nereids – fifty of them living in the Mediterranean; and both live on in the custom of the human girls who bathed, before their wedding, in the purifying waters.

31

H

Previous page: Juno discovers Jupiter with Io (a painting by
Pieter Lastman, 1583–1633)
Below: Sheila-na-Gig, Celtic goddess of creation and
destruction, surprisingly found in a Herefordshire Church
Right: A dominating red demon from Japan – Nikko, image of
the Sun; *inset*, Hotei Osho, a Buddhist priest-god, known in
Europe as Pusa

The Celts

The gods and goddesses of the Celts seem most often to have been provincials, belonging to one tribe or another, and locally worshipped. There were exceptions, like Epona, the horse-goddess worshipped in Italy, Spain and eastern Europe, and undoubtedly in Britain, where the huge and handsome horses carved into the chalk of hillsides (the finest specimen is at Uffington in Berkshire) probably pay tribute to her cult.

One of the most important Celtic gods was the Irish Dagda – Eochaid Ollathair, Father of All. An unimposing figure, plump and ugly and dressed as a peasant, he was sufficiently strong nevertheless to use a club so large that it had to be transported on a cart, into which it was lifted by eight men. With one end of his club the Dagda reduced his enemies to carcasses, but with the other end he could resurrect them. He was an accomplished harpist and had some warm-hearted traits, for he carefully made use of a bottomless pot from which endless quantities of food were drawn and given away to the needy. The Dagda seems to have been a man of conspicuous appetites. He married twice, and one of his most authentically recorded feats was the consumption of an inordinate amount of porridge (drawn from a hole in the ground), after which he made love vigorously to a passing maiden. The anecdote reinforces his position as a fertility god.

The Dagda was a god of the Tuatha dé Danaan, or People of Danu, who allegedly occupied Ireland in ancient times. Another of their gods was Lug, whose cult spread as far as Spain and Switzerland. Lug turned up at the gates of the royal palace of Nuada, King of the Tuatha, to ask for a job. He was, he said, a carpenter; but when he heard there was a carpenter at court already, he claimed to be a harpist – then, in turn, a poet, an historian, a hero, a magician, an astrologer, a cook, and a great many other things. He deserved his name Samildánach, meaning 'of many skills'. Lug was extremely accurate with the sling – he killed the one-eyed giant Balor with one – and seems eventually to have supplanted the Dagda as guardian of the Tuatha.

The other gods of the Tuatha are less individual. Among them are Nuanda the King and keeper of the great sword of his people; Gobniu the blacksmith and brewer; and Ogma the champion fighter.

The goddess Danu, foundress of the Tuatha, is a shadowy figure, one of whose names seems to have been Brigid, and she survived as St Brigit in the Christian calendar. More is known about Macha, who while pregnant was forced by the Ulstermen to run a race against a team of horses. She gave birth to twins, and died cursing the warriors of Ulster, who ever afterwards at critical moments of a battle would find themselves suffering the pangs of women in childbirth.

The Irish myths of Nuatha travelled easily across the sea to Wales, and spread thence into England, where King Nuada reappeared as King Ludd, and the People of Danu became the Children of Donn. An individual god did appear in the person of Gwydion, a valiant fighter, fine poet and expert magician; and perhaps the most notable, peculiarly Welsh god was Bendegeit Bran, an enormous giant

THE LADY OF THE LAKE
TELLETH ARTHVR OF THE
SWORD EXCALIBVR

who possessed a cauldron which could restore the dead to life. He was quite capable of wading across the Irish Sea without getting his feet too wet, and indeed did so. A useful attribute of his was an ability to lie down and form a living bridge across wide rivers. He was finally killed by a poisoned arrow, and as he lay dying he ordered his head to be cut off and placed on a hill in London to frighten off attacking foreigners.

On the question of whether we can seriously consider King Arthur an immortal in the strict sense of the word, one feels hesitant. He was almost certainly a real person, but his life and exploits have become legends as strong as any of those of the gods of Greece. They are shot through with miraculous visions and strange events, and have at least one unquestionable immortal whose presence enlivens them: Merlin, the magician. He was said to have been fathered by the Devil, but was himself wise and good and an invaluable aid to Arthur against his enemies, especially against his son Modred, the result of an incestuous liaison between the King and his half-sister, the evil Morgan le Fay. Merlin is still occasionally to be heard, if not seen, in a cave beneath the ruined castle at Tintagel, in Cornwall, said to have been Arthur's birth-place.

The marvellous chronicle of King Arthur's adventures is set down in *Le Morte Darthur*, a prose translation from the French made by Sir Thomas Malory in the fifteenth century, and first printed by Caxton in 1485. Half of it is taken up by the knightly quest for the Holy Grail, the cup used by Jesus at the last supper. This is a major factor in English myth, and it is dealt with in very early English poetry. It was thought for some centuries that Joseph of Arimathea might have brought the cup to England, and the area around Glastonbury, Somerset, is particularly taken up with that legend and the legend that Jesus as a child might have journeyed to the British Isles.

The strongest element in English myth is, however, that of the smaller immortal – the fairy, elf and goblin. Whether or not these were ever genuine fantasies has recently been opened to question by speculation that the Little People may have been visitors from other planets, the toadstools with which they are much associated having been space-ships on their legs or pedestals. But to ponder on this would be to concern oneself with other, more modern myths, and immortals of another kind.

The Teutons

The Teutons originated in the lands between the Oder and Vistula rivers, roughly in the areas of Poland and Czechoslovakia (where they were known as the Goths), in the Scandinavian countries, and in West Germany (the ancestors of the present Germans, and of the Anglo-Saxons who eventually established themselves in Britain, and spread southward to the Rhine and the Danube). So in speaking of Teutonic myths one covers a mythology which, though it perhaps grew up in a relatively small area, was carried over a large part of Europe. It was not an original mythology if indeed any mythological system was. Some stories from India, from Greece, Ireland, Rome and the East have their part in it, often heavily disguised. It grew and developed until Christianity came to strike the immortals of the Teutons a blow from which they survived in a less satisfactory state than the immortals of Greece and Rome.

According to the ancient bards of Iceland, the first of the immortals was Ymir, father of giants. He was murdered (like the Greek Cronus) by his great-grandsons; his flesh became the land, his blood the sea, his bones the mountains and his hair the trees. Odin, Vili and Ve, the three great-grandsons, built three palaces in the Land of Asgard, with a useful connecting bridge, Bifröst, to Middle Earth, where earthlings lived. There were two other regions of the known universe – Jotunheim, where the giants dwelt, and Hel, the land of the dead. They clustered under the shelter of the branches of Yggdrasill, the World Tree, an ash which towered at the centre of the universe.

It is difficult to provide a comprehensive guide to the Teutonic gods, for unlike Olympia with its twelve (or thirteen) immortal personalities, various Teutonic tribes had their own ideas about the supernatural establishment; some of the gods appear in various guises, and it is easy to confuse them, one with another. There were, however, three gods unquestionably at the head of the hierarchy: Woden, Donar and Tiw (their names had variants, but those were perhaps the most common renderings).

Woden was the leading god of the pantheon, the ancestor of all earthly kings, the god invoked before battle (before, for instance, the Anglo-Saxon invasion of Britain), and the god whose name we still commemorate every time we awake on a Wednesday or Woden's-day morning. Woden at first was a god of the night, magical ruler of the land of the dead, who thundered through the black sky at the head of an army of dead warriors, dressed in his great flowing cloak and broad-brimmed hat. He rose to become supreme commander of the gods, no longer riding at the head of his army, but preferring to remain on his throne in his great hall, Valhalla, invoking the spirits of heroism and self-sacrifice, deciding the outcome of earthly wars, and dispensing rewards. A cruel god, he demanded both animal and human sacrifice; tattered bodies, clothed only in the rags of their skins, hung in the branches of trees near his battlefields.

In the north, his name became Odin, and his character perhaps softened somewhat: he was a handsome and intelligent soldier-poet, sharing with his distant relative Zeus the ability to change at a moment into any one of a hundred forms. He made the laws, and conceived the custom that all a warrior's belongings should be burned on the funeral-pyre with his body, so that he could enjoy them when he was reborn into the select company in Valhalla. Odin possessed the most fleet of all horses, the fabulous Sleipnir, never outrun by any other animal; but as time went by rode out less and less frequently, relying on his two ravens, Hugin and Munin (Thought and Memory), to tell him everything that went on in Middle Earth.

Odin really combines the personalities of many gods: apart from his adeptness in martial and literary arts, he was also amorous. His wife Frigg

39

Left: Thor battles with the Midgard, the fearful sea-serpent
(Henry Fuseli, 1741–1825)
Below: A Victorian artist's impression of a scene from Wagner's
Ring: Wotan invokes the magic fire to guard Brünnhilde as she
sleeps

(sometimes named, or perhaps confused with,
Freyja, who may or may not have been the same
goddess) grumbled at his many adventures, though
she herself seems not to have had an impeccable
moral character. Odin was especially fond of one
earthly family, the Volsungs, whose saga is related
in *Die Walküre*, the second opera of the *Ring*,
Wagner's great four-opera cycle on the subject of
the Teutonic gods. One of the most spectacular
of Odin's actions was his apparent act of self-
destruction, when he hung himself in the branches
of the World Tree, mortally wounded by his own
spear. After nine days he saw beneath him a set of
mysterious runes or tablets, reached down for them,
and found – it was what he had gambled on – that
they renewed his life, making him a true immortal.

The Teutonic god of thunder was Donar or Thor,
the wheels of whose chariot could be heard
rumbling across the roof of the universe.
Occasionally he would hurl his thunderbolt at the
world below him, in an access of rage or irritability.
The Norwegians and Germans specially revered
him, and he is related to both Jupiter and Hercules
in Roman mythology.

The Norse poets have drawn the most thorough
portrait of Thor, as a simple soldier, forthright,
brave and determined. He seems in fact to have been
the favourite god of the ordinary soldier rather than
of the great hero: while the latter was under the
protection of Odin, Thor looked after the
infantryman – the poor clod swept into fighting by
the force of circumstance. 'Odin has the nobles who
fall in battle; Thor has the peasants', as one of the
Eddas, an early Norse poem, puts it. In battle, Thor
behaved with all the fury of a rash commando,
shouting at the top of his voice, and hurling his tall,
solid body towards the foe, preceded by his bristling
red beard, and swinging his immortal hammer
around his head. In addition to the hammer he had
two other valuable weapons: a pair of iron gloves
which would never let go of its handle, and a girdle
which doubled his strength the moment he put it on.
His miraculous powers were severely practical:
when he went out on his belligerent rampages round
the world, he travelled not behind a quartet of noble
stallions, but in a cart drawn by two he-goats (relics,
perhaps, of the time centuries earlier when he had
been exclusively god of the earth, agriculture and
fair weather). Strong beasts, the goats never let him
down – once drawing him to the entrance of Hel
itself. At the end of the day, if he felt hungry, he

killed and ate them, carefully setting aside the hides.
In the morning, when he touched them with his
hammer, the skins would stand up and become once
more two living goats, ready to proceed with the
journey.

Thor had a faithful wife, Sif (celebrated for her
bright hair), and was faithful to her. They were the
parents of several children, the sons as strong as
Thor himself. Apart from being courageous, he was
game for any adventure, and once went down to
Jotunheim disguised as a woman to woo the giant
Thrym, who had stolen his magic hammer. He
almost gave himself away at Thrym's palace, sitting
down at table to eat everything in sight – a whole ox,
eight large salmon, and a variety of bits and pieces.

But Thrym was delighted by this evidently lusty maiden, and brought the hammer to her: upon which Thor seized it, killing Thrym and escaping safely. On another occasion he hooked the World Serpent, the dreadful Midgard, while out fishing. God and beast stared implacably into each other's eyes for one fierce moment before the monster broke away and sank back into the unimaginable depths of the sea, to emerge only once more as the gods' reign ended.

The adventures of Thor, often accompanied by the quick-talking Loki acting as his guide and adviser, are among the most delightful and absorbing of world myths. Tiw, the Scandinavian god of the sky, is by comparison rather dull: a god of law, outshone by Donar, seen mainly as an equivalent of the Roman Jupiter and the Greek Zeus, his name survives in Tues-day. Loki, a minor god, one of the most brilliant and equivocal of all immortals, completely overshadows him.

Loki is akin to several Greek gods, with his endless talent to amuse, his demonaic attributes, his sly sense of humour and his non-stop chattering. While he ostensibly supported his superiors, he never stopped working to discomfit them, and frequently succeeded. Though he plays a major part in *Das Rheingold*, the first opera of the *Ring*, he is not a German god, but Scandinavian. He was in the first place a fire-demon, who became a blood-brother of Odin. There is no doubt that he could charm the other gods off their thrones, and very often charmed the goddesses too; an inveterate seducer, he was handsome, witty and irresistible. He was also capable of double-dealing on a grand scale, betraying even Thor himself. His malice finally overflowed on the occasion of a celebrated banquet which Aegir, a giant and Lord of the Seas, held for all the gods and goddesses while Thor was away. Loki was not invited. By now he had succeeded in upsetting everyone, and Aegir had rightly decided that he would be a skeleton at the feast. But just as the merry-making was getting under way, the doors of the hall flew open, and there stood Loki, demanding a place at the table. The gods felt that perhaps they should not deny him, and Odin his blood-brother cast the final vote in his favour. A place was found and a cup brought. But no sooner had Loki sat down, than he began a tirade of abuse, recalling all the most scandalous affairs in which he had acted as go-between for the other gods, betraying confidence after confidence, secret after

secret. When he had demolished the reputation of every god, he started on the goddesses.

The faithful Sif, Thor's wife, came to him with a cup of mead, pleading with him to be quiet. His response was to claim that he himself had held her naked and acquiescent in his arms – Sif, the most faithful and innocent of them all. As soon as he mentioned her husband's name, however, there was an ominous roll of thunder – the sound of the wheels of Thor's approaching chariot. Although the great god had occasionally invoked Loki's help, he had also suffered under his tongue; and no doubt he remembered, too, the occasion when Loki had stolen Sif's marvellous head of bright hair. Before the threat of the magic hammer, Loki backed away, but as he left he prophesied the *Götterdämmerung*, the downfall of the gods and of their whole hierarchy.

Of the other gods, only a few were characters of real individuality, among whom certainly was Balder, a god of light – Odin's son by the goddess Frigg. He was a cheerful youth, outstandingly handsome and loved by everyone – except, of course, the egregious Loki, who indeed eventually arranged Balder's murder. He had premonitions of apprehension and gloom, and to cheer him up his mother organized an agreement in which everything on earth – stones, water, animals, metals – swore never to harm him. But Loki discovered that she had forgotten one thing: mistletoe. One day when the other gods, in play, were pelting Balder with everything to hand, for the fun of seeing how the missiles shied away from his inviolable skin at the last possible moment, he picked a sharp mistletoe twig and handed it to Balder's blind brother Höd. Höd was as horrified as everyone else when his brother dropped dead. His wife Nanna died of grief, and the whole of nature mourned – an event commemorated after every winter, when the melting of frost, snow and ice represents the tears of the world for the dead god.

The gods did not give up their dead brother without a struggle. They managed to persuade Hel, the goddess who ruled over the underworld which bore her name, to give him up if everyone on earth shed tears for him. But one ill-tempered giantess refused, and for the time being Balder remained in Hel.

Heimdall was another god of light, who held much the same position in Asgard as the Roman

Janus and the Indian Vaynu held in their respective myths. Tall and handsome, he had teeth of pure gold, slept only as long as a bird, could see in the dark, and had hearing so acute that he could hear the grass grow, or the wool on a sheep's back.

Njörd, Frey and Freyja, the three Vanir, belonged to another race than the Aesir – the race of which Thor and his friends and relations were members. While the latter were warlike and belligerent, the Vanir were quiet, peaceable and benevolent – at their best in the warm summer months, specially fond of relaxation, gods of farming and peaceful commerce. There was once a fierce war between the two races, but the Vanir proved surprisingly victorious, and a somewhat uneasy peace prevailed afterwards.

Njörd, in his youth, seems to have been a goddess, under the name Nerthus. After his sex-change, he settled into a home at Noatun, by the sea; this led to some altercation with his wife Skadi, who preferred the hills. They had never been compatible. Skadi had been offered the choice of one of the gods for a husband, but had had to choose on the evidence of their bare feet alone. She had a passion for Balder, and chose the best-formed feet on show. They turned out to be Njörd's. While she was disappointed, she went through with the marriage, but when the pair disagreed about the site for their home, she decided to go back to her hunting in the hills, while Njörd remained by the seashore, where he could hear the mermaids calling, each to each. It was an amiable liaison.

Frey was their son, and became one of the most popular gods in all Teutonic mythology, with grand temples and a widespread cult (in which, however, human sacrifice played a part). His personality was imposing; his chariot was drawn by a golden boar, made for him by two clever dwarfs. Other dwarfs made him a ship, the *Skipbladnir*, almost as fleet as his chariot; certainly no other ship could catch it. In it he could carry all the Aesir, yet when not in use it folded handily to pocket size.

Other minor gods – Bragi, the god of poetry, Hoenir the handsome (but, like Ajax, with no more brain than ear-wax), Vali and Vidar, two sons of Odin – were matched by goddesses, the leader of whom was Freyja, twin sister of Frey, and so beautiful that everyone who saw her desired her. A number of gods and men achieved their ambition in that regard; she was a generally immoral goddess, obtaining her famous necklace, for one, by spending the night with each of the four dwarfs who made it.

The *Götterdämmerung*, or Twilight of the Gods, which Wagner described in music much more graphic than any words, is the most tragic of all myths, a painful story of glory crashing in ruins, told in the *Voluspa*, one of the finest of the prose *Eddas* of the twelfth century or earlier. Loki, as might be expected, was heavily involved; but the gods brought the end of their civilization upon themselves. They had employed a giant to build them a magnificent palace, and when the work was completed, asked Loki to devise a trick to make it unnecessary to pay him. Loki was delighted to do so, but the result was that everyone lost faith in the good name of the gods. Mortals, taking advantage of the bad example shown them, began to dishonour their oaths and contracts, and an age of deceit was born. The murder of Balder brought things to a head. Beside his body the Aesir swore an oath of revenge. War broke out throughout the whole world, and was waged in an ice age during which winter lasted the whole year.

Giants, immensely powerful wolves, the inhabitants of the underworld and the Valkyries (Odin's fierce women messengers) all took part in the conflict. The notorious World Serpent, the Midgard, rose for the second time from the depths of the sea, and after a fierce fight was killed by Thor, but not until its poison had caught hold of him so that he himself died just afterwards.

With the defeat of Tyr at the teeth of Garm, the

hound of hell, the last of the gods died. Without them, man was helpless: the world began to lose its shape, to become distorted; stars slithered from their places in the sky, and the giant Surt set fire to the world. Flames spouted from long-extinct volcanoes and deep fissures, so that even the fastest-flowing rivers drifted away in steam. Finally the sea broke over the bare earth to drown the last traces of the homes of giants, gods and men.

Very slowly the seas sank back, the rivers returned to their beds, the earth was covered with a fresh down of green, and once more a race of gods was born – leading them, miraculously, the beloved Balder, reborn to sit rather sadly with his brother Höd in a palace built from the ruins of Odin's Valhalla. Two sons of Odin, two of Bor and two of Thor completed the new pantheon. Gradually men, too, crept from the wreckage of the former earth, and began to breed and increase. But things were never the same as in the great days of Asgard, when the world and the gods were young.

Below: The Finnish hero Vainamoinen, son of the Virgin of the Air, tries to seize his promised bride Aino; but to avoid him, she becomes a water-sprite
Opposite: A Russian peasant's carving of a powerfully protective anonymous god

The North

Jumala, Father of the Gods in the mythology of the northern countries of Finland, Estonia and Lapland, was one of those all-powerful but vague gods whose personality remained unresolved, and who was eventually succeeded by a more individual immortal – in this case by Ukko, god of the sky and the air, who supported the world and in turn was supported by Paive (the Sun), Kuu (the Moon), Otava (the Great Bear) and Ilma (the Air).

Ilma's daughter Luonnotar grew, after many centuries, weary of her virginity, lept into the sea and was fertilized by the waves. The world as we know it sprang, however, not directly from her, but from a clutch of eggs laid by a duck on her left knee (the only part of her at that time to be seen above the water). When they hatched out, the top halves of their shells became the heavens, the lower halves the earth, the yolks the sun and the whites the moon.

The gods of the fields and woods (Pellervoinen and Tapio) were, with Ahto and his wife Vellamo, the water-immortals, perhaps the most important of the minor gods. Ahto was not a prepossessing creature, living as he did in the depths of a pool of black slime, and being generally bad-tempered and apt to attack humans. There were other unpleasant spirits, too – among them Lempo, Paha and Hiisi, who were familiar with Tuonela, the Finnish land of the dead, and could pass through the loathsome river and past Surma, the guardian monster, which protected it. Tuoni and his wife Tuonetar ruled there, aided by their daughters Kipu-Tytto, spirit of sickness, and Loviatar, the source of all evil, with her black pocked face and her nine children, who included Gout, Ulcers and Scabies. It was Tuonetar's habit to welcome newcomers to hell with a tankard of beer full of frogs and worms.

Slavonia

The mythology of the Slavonic people is a rough and simple one, with its roots in the peasant life led by the farmers and hunters who ranged the open country of central and eastern Europe. The conflict between the forces of good and evil was again at the heart of it, personified by the White God and the Black God – Byelobog and Chernobog: white and black, sunlight and darkness. It cannot be said that either Byelobog or Chernobog had very strongly developed characters. The former was spoken of as an old man dressed in white clothes, who roamed about the country doing works of kindness – finding lost pots, or curing sick horses, placing a far beast in the line of the hunter's shot, or ensuring a good crop.

The sun, moon and stars were also personified: Dazhbog, the Sun, and Svarogich, Fire, were the children of Svarog, the Sky – the father of all things. Fire, which had come to earth at a moment of inspiration, straight from the Sky himself, as lightning, was venerated as being especially valuable, to the extent that man was forbidden to curse while the domestic fire was being lit. According to the Poles, Dazhbog's home in the east was a paradise of milk and honey from which he rode out every morning in a golden chariot with diamond wheels drawn by twelve fire-breathing white horses. The Serbs saw him as an upright and handsome young king, though according to some myths he grew steadily older as the day wore on, to die in the evening as a red-faced and bloated elderly gentleman. He ruled, the Russians believed, over the twelve kingdoms of the zodiacal signs, and was served by two beautiful girls – two Auroras – and by the seven planets, as well as by seven immortal messengers (comets with blazing tails). His old, bald Uncle Myesyats (the Moon) stood by to advise him.

Myesyats in other variations of the story was a young girl who married the Sun in summer, left him in winter, and returned in the spring. The Sun and she were father and mother of the stars, and when they had marital differences, caused earthquakes. In Ukrainia, they changed sexes, the Moon being the husband and the Sun his wife.

The Auroras – the dawn and the evening, sometimes joined by a third Aurora, Midnight – were for a while very important as owners of a god chained up to a limb of the Great Bear constellation. Should the chain ever break, the end of the world would be at hand. Sometimes the Auroras were helped by two stars, Zvezda Dennitsa and Vechernyaya Zvezda, whose special task was to groom the white horses of the Sun. There also sprang up from time to time minor gods whose writ ran only for short periods and in specific areas: gods of the winds, for instance – sometimes as many as seven of them.

The Earth as an individual god was often addressed and invoked as an upright and honest judge, called to confirm the honesty of witnesses in land disputes, for example. But she never took on a very distinct personality.

The minor immortals of the Slavonic people included, as usual, malevolent (or at least mischievous) creatures like the Domovoi, resembling the Pan of Greece or the Puck of Britain: short, thickset, covered in hair, sometimes with horns and a tail – but more usually, according to peasant lore, looking like an animated stook of hay. Apparently when the universe was created, a group of malcontent spirits staged a revolt against Svarog, whereupon they were driven from his presence, falling like autumn leaves through the thin air of the newly created earth, some coming to ground in backyards, some down chimneys, some into forests and some on to the plains. They were each 'Domovoi', each had the same characteristics: but at least gradually as the centuries passed they became somewhat domesticated, and served man, as well as (sometimes) tricking him. Slav spirits of this type share the strange capacity to be at once one and many, singular and plural.

Less approachable than the Domovoi, and shyer, were the Dvorovoi, who generally lived in outhouses or farm buildings, and the spirits of the farmyard, best appeased if animals were not to suffer. White-feathered or -furred animals and birds were safe – and, presumably, blondes, for one Dvorovoi is known to have fallen violently in love with a dark-haired human girl, ordering her never to comb out her hair, which he had plaited. When she in turn fell in love with a human man, she combed out the plaits – and was found strangled on her wedding morning.

The Bannik, spirit of the baths, was felt if you stuck your naked back out of the bath-house: if the future was to be pleasant, he stroked you, if unpleasant, you felt his nails across your spine. The Leshy, spirit of the woodlands, and the Polevik, spirit of the fields, were worth consulting; and the gods of war (Svantovit and Pyerun, Zroya – a virgin war-goddess – and Volos) and of peace (Yarilo and Kupala) were invoked in turn.

Black Africa

The mythology of Black Africa, despite the fact that it arose out of the legends and stories invented by the members of well over six thousand separate tribes, almost always has at its centre one often rather vague god, the creator of the world – known as Ndriananahary in Madagascar, Cagn to the bushmen, Nzame among the Fan of the Congo, Nyamia among the Agni of Indene, in Guinea. The names are almost as varied as the tribes, but the concept is much the same, and there is one supreme god, 'The Everlasting One', or 'He who roars so loud that the people are terror-struck'.

In general, the great god must not be irritated by the prayers of earthlings: he is far too important. Apart from anything else, it may be impolitic for man to remind him of his presence, for (as in Christian myth) man and woman displeased God not too long after he had created them, and were thrown out of the beautiful garden in which they originally made their home. The reasons for his displeasure are not always very clear, though the woman is usually held to blame. In Nigeria, it is said that she annoyed God by constantly knocking at the sky, the floor of his house, with a stick; in the Congo, she simply nagged him so hard that he lowered her down to earth in a bucket to torment men.

The Masai of south-east Africa ascribe the population of the world to a divine woman – daughter of 'Ng ai, the god. One man originally lived alone on earth – Kintu, who was very handsome and was selected as her husband by 'Ng ai's daughter. She persuaded her father to invite Kintu to heaven, and to set him a number of tests, which with her help he successfully completed. They were married, but her brother Death took exception to not being invited to the wedding, and has since persisted in killing all their children.

The Pahouin of the Congo believed that God originally modelled man of clay in the shape of a lizard which he placed in a pond. After seven days, the lizard emerged shaped like a man. The Cameroons remembered how God had made the earth, and then came down to make four sons: N'Kokon, the intellectual; Otukut, the dull-witted; Ngi, the gorilla; and Wo, the chimpanzee. Muluku, god of the Macouas of Mozambique, originally made two races – men and monkeys. The latter behaved so well, and were so hard-working and intelligent in contrast to mankind, that Muluku cut off their tails, attached them to men, and swopped the races round.

49

The Shilluk of the White Nile charmingly invented a creation myth which explained the different shades of colour in man's skin. Juok, the creator, found white earth in the land of the white man, making the Egyptian from mud from the Nile and the Shilluk from black earth. He made man with two arms, incidentally, so that one could pull up weeds and the other use the hoe.

Bumba, god of the Bushongo of the Congo, simply vomited up the sun, moon, stars and eight kinds of animals, from which the living species developed by natural selection. Earth and heaven were originally man and wife and lived at peace; but later they had a quarrel, and a divorce was arranged.

Cagn, the god of the bushmen of Hereroland, had a wife, Coti, and two sons, Zogaz and Gewi. They never attempted to explain how man was created, but many adventures were related of the gods themselves: how Cagn used the birds as messengers, and could change his shoes into dogs to attack his enemies; how he could turn ill-mannered men into monkeys, and himself into any kind of animal. (This misfired on one occasion, when he was actually killed by man and his body eaten by ants, all by mistake. Fortunately, his bones joined up again, and Cagn became himself once more.)

Sometimes the creation myths go some way towards explaining the otherwise surprising fact that one half of the world (the white half) apparently prospered to an unbelievable extent, while the black half lived in comparative or complete poverty. In the Congo, the Pahouin believed that God originally lived in the centre of Africa, with three sons – a black man, a white man and a gorilla. The black man and the gorilla were so disobedient that God left them and went to live on the coast with his white son; the gorilla vanished into the forests; and the black man and his descendants ever afterwards lived in poverty.

The people of south-west Madagascar told how Ndriananahary one day sent his son Ataokoloinona ('The Strange Thing, Water') down to the bare earth to survey it and propose a use for it. He found the world a desert, and, scorched by the heat, he burrowed deep into the earth and was never seen again. After some centuries, Ndriananahary was forced to create a race of men and send them to earth in search of his son. They never found him – which was not surprising, for the earth was so barren that most of their energy was taken up in trying to grow enough food to stay alive. From time to time they were forced to send one of their number up to Ndriananahary to beg him for help. These messengers never returned, and it was soon said of them that they were 'dead'. But Ndriananahary did send occasional rain to earth as a reward for man's enternal search for Ataokoloinona.

As in most cultures, many African tribes invented stories to account for the presence in the sky of the sun and moon, and the difference between them. Some people of the Zambesi suppose that the Moon was originally extremely envious of the Sun's brilliance, and while the latter was on his nightly visit to the underworld, stole some of his bright feathers. When the Sun returned, he was so angry that he threw a handful of mud at the Moon, which can still be seen sticking to her otherwise fair face. But every ten years the Moon got her own back by throwing mud at the Sun. Sometimes it showed as spots, and sometimes it completely obscured his face; but he soon managed to wipe it off. (This was an easy and surprising way of explaining the phenomena of sunspots and eclipses.)

Some tribesmen of the Zambesi once attempted to climb up to the sun to kill it, but did not succeed. The Bambala of the Congo set up an enormous pole on which they hoped to reach the moon, curious to find out what it was made of; but the pole fell down before they got there. In a legend of the Lower Congo, the story of the sun throwing mud at the moon recurs; when as a result the moon shone less brightly, there was a great flood, during which men were changed into monkeys and women into lizards.

The Bomitaba of the Congo believed that the sun and moon were originally two suns; but this proved impossible for man to tolerate – the dry heat drove him to distraction. So one day it was suggested that the two suns should bathe; one threw himself into a river, the other only pretended. The wet sun was put out by the water, and emerged as the moon, shining quite brightly, but coldly.

The Serera of Senegambia explain the difference between sun and moon in another way. The Sun's mother and the Moon's mother were once bathing naked in a waterfall. The Sun modestly averted his eyes, while the Moon looked curiously on. After the bath, the Sun's mother congratulated him on his modesty, and promised that she would arrange with God that as a tribute to it, no man would ever be able to look straight at his face. But the Moon's

Left: Before sacrificing to Ogun, god of iron, a tribesman of a Nigerian region dances, masked, before his image
Centre: The Oba-Ohe of Benin, Nigeria, attended by two slaves, was possessed by Oloku, god of the great waters; a great chief, he was worshipped as late as the seventeenth century
Right: Man becomes god: a hunter, with gun at his hip, is elevated as a god in a memorial erected by the Galla tribe in Ethiopia

mother told her sternly that her immodesty would be rewarded by the arrangement that any man could stare at her for ever without flinching or looking away.

A Ugandan tribe tells how the Sun and Moon decided to get rid of their children, and planned to kill them all. But while the Sun carried out his threat, the Moon had second thoughts – which explains why the Sun reigns alone in the sky, while the Moon is still surrounded by her vast family of stars.

Spirits of good and evil abound in Black African mythology, the spirits of evil on the whole being the most colourful. The Negroes of Madagascar believe that the Razanes, good spirits who are the souls of their ancestors, are hindered by Angatch, the evil spirit. The Macouas and Banayis of Mozambique know that Muluku the good god is opposed by Minepa, the Devil. Heitsi-Eibib, god of the Hottentots (who himself is prone to fits of bad temper, and during one of them cursed the lion, which originally lived in trees, so that it had to come down to earth), has a violent opponent in Gaunab, maker of the rainbow. In Masai myth the rainbow is also evil, and at one time tried to swallow the world.

The Pahouin have an especially unpleasant evil spirit, Ngworekara, who rules over the spirits of the dead – spirits of an ugliness equal to his own, with lank, sparse hair, long, dirty ears, and mouths like the trunks of elephants.

The spirits of the dead play an important part in

most African myths. After death, the Pahouin
believe, bad spirits wander in space with no other
occupation than tormenting the living and eating
their hearts. The Bomitaba of the Congo speak of
the Mokadi or spirits of the dead having power over
the living. Among the Agni of Indene and Sanwi, in
Guinea, Kaka-Guia, the bull-headed, escorts spirits
to Nyamia the great god, who can order them to
protect particular villages on earth. The people of
Dahomey believe in specialist spirits, Legba and Fa,
who attach themselves to individual men; similarly,
Wokolo is a devil who can also make a set against a
particular man.

The invention of a reason for death is especially
ingenious in many tribes. The Masai of
Mozambique tell how god taught Le-eyo, his
favourite man, to pronounce, when a child died, the
formula 'Man dies and returns: the moon dies and
does not return'. But one day Le-eyo failed to do so,
and the opposite became true. The Zulus remember
how Unkulunkulu, the first man and supreme god,
sent the chameleon to announce to man his
immortality. But the chameleon took his time –
stopping, some say, to eat; others, to sleep in the sun
– and meanwhile God changed his mind and sent a
lizard, who reached man first and pronounced the
message 'Man shall die!' Though the chameleon
eventually got round to delivering his message, no
one believed him; and indeed he turned out to be
wrong.

The Ubangui of the Congo believe that death is

53

never natural: it is always caused by some evil spirit, or by another person – and the spirits of the dead spend much time revenging themselves on the murderers. In the first place, God generally seemed to intend that man should be immortal, but some accident or design prevented it. Libanza, god of the Upotos of the Congo, sent one day for the people of the moon and the people of the earth, for instance. The moon-men came running, and in reward for their promptness Libanza promised that they should only die for two days in each month. But when the earth-men eventually strolled in, he was so furious with them for their casualness that he promised them death; and after it they would appear before him, to be disposed of as he willed.

The tribes on the shores of Lake Kivu remember how jealous Death, always kept at bay, one day managed to steal a woman while God was away. The woman was disinclined to remain his prisoner, and began to rise from her grave. The earth began to shift, but was seen by her daughter-in-law, who poured boiling water on her, remarking: 'What is dead should stay dead!' When God got back from his trip, he noticed the woman's absence, and hearing the story went furiously in search of Death, who hid from him in the belly of an old woman. God discovered this, and decided that since the old woman was past child-bearing, it would be worthwhile to kill her, extract Death, and deal with him. But a girl came out of an adjacent hut just as

God was cutting the old woman's throat, and Death escaped into her body: at which point God gave up, and decided that since humans kept giving Death refuge, he might as well stay with them.

In Uganda, it was a dog who brought death: the Nandi tell how it was sent with news of immortality, but was so discourteously received that it lost its temper and proclaimed mortality instead. A dog, too, was sent to God, requesting that man could be reborn after death. A frog, on the other hand, took it into his head to go to God with the plea that death should be the end of man. The dog stopped off for some food, and the frog got to God first. Receiving two opposite requests, God decided to grant that of the first-comer.

Animals and birds are untrustworthy messengers, evidently. The Gallas, on the other hand, believe that a bird was sent by God to advise man, when he got old, simply to slough off his skin and become young again. But the bird met a snake on the way, and gave it God's message instead, in exchange for a piece of meat.

Most African peoples believe in survival after death, however, and that the spirits of the dead are extremely potent in the exercise of magic. They are often to be found attached to animals or plants or even stones, and the worship of the spirits of ancestors and relatives is extremely prevelent. The Madagascans believe that the souls of chiefs enter the bodies of crocodiles, and those of ordinary people into lynxes. When a Mozambique chief died, as in Egypt and China living slaves would be buried with him to serve him in the next world.

Bad spirits are often more potent than good, and in many cases prayers were more vigorously addressed to them for that reason. They often work furiously under fear of damnation. The Pahouin believed that the evil god Ngworekara has total power over the spirits under his command, who lurk in forests or on mountain-tops (the feeling of dizziness one gets in high places is caused by the spirits who live there) waiting to waylay innocent men.

The Mundanga of the Congo, almost alone, believed that animals have individual souls just as men and women do. When a living thing died, its soul entered a deep cave in the earth, where it took the body of a female to create a new being – woman giving birth to a human being, an animal to an animal.

55

Rome

In strong contrast to the Greek gods, with their endless, often disreputable adventures, the gods of Rome seem rather to be administrators, generally concerned with the work with which they are associated, and with little time to spare for extramural activities. While the Greek gods had the time and energy to reflect their subjects' human weaknesses, failings and pleasures, the Roman gods were kept hard at work seeing to their worshippers' practical needs – helping them by encouraging the crops to grow, ensuring their wives' fertility, and aiding them in battle. The truth is, too, that they were far less individual than their Greek counterparts – and far less original, for they often owed their personalities to the myths of other countries and other religions. The Roman religion itself was a sort of amalgam of practises from Greece, Syria, Persia, Egypt and elsewhere, patched together to form a system which would best serve the Roman people. It was an extremely down-to-earth religion, too – the gods were made for man, rather than man for the gods, which is why Mars rose so quickly to pre-eminence. Mars was first the god of agriculture, so important to the prosperity of Rome, and then of war, so vital to the expansion of the empire.

Mars was important, too, as the father of Romulus and Remus. The son of Juno (his father was in the remarkable guise of a flower), Mars seduced the vestal virgin Rhea Silvia while she was asleep, and twin sons were the result. They were suckled by a wolf, as is well known, and were led by a flight of birds to the site of a new city, the boundaries of which Romulus laid down, consolidating his right to the ground by killing his brother, who trespassed on what was to be the site of Rome.

Mars at first lived in the woods and hills, overseeing farming. It was only much later that he became the god of war, with a temple at Rome where sacrifices were made to ensure victory, after which he expected a share of the loot. Occasionally, as an infantryman, he appeared on the battlefield itself; and as the Roman Empire spread, his temples – in conquered lands as well as in the vicinity of Rome – became more and more numerous. He was a particular patron of the horse, and in March (the month which bears his name) and October there were special races held on the Campus Martius – the field of Mars – after which the unfortunate winning team was sacrificed. It was at the Campus Martius that the Roman infantry paraded, and there stood the earliest known Martian altar. Out on the Appian Way was another temple, where the army assembled each year to form a martial procession which paraded through the city.

The Emperor Augustus was particularly devoted to Mars, building him many temples. These were mostly outside the city, where his influence would do most good to the land. When Augustus recovered the Roman standards lost in Parthia by Crassus, he placed them in Mars' temple. As to the mythology, the anecdotes told about him are frequently those associated, in Greece, with Ares, a much less handsome and appealing immortal.

The Romans looked upon their own god Janus, one of the few uniquely Roman gods, as creator of the world. He was god of all buildings, especially their entrances and exits (in English-speaking

countries such as the United States the word 'janitor' is used in preference to 'porter'). Janus was also the god of beginnings, and it was for that reason he was supposed to have presided over the making of the world. The doors of his temples were left open to signify the starting of new wars or campaigns.

Janus had two faces (he may once, indeed, have had four), the better to keep watch from his various doorways. But his capacity for seeing too many ways at once did make him somewhat muddled, and may be associated with the chaos which existed before the world's creation and which he also represented. As Father of the Gods and head of a cult which Romulus himself seemed to have initiated, Janus (whose name is commemorated in the first month of the European year) took precedence even over Jupiter, god of the sky – the sun and moon and all the heavenly bodies. Jupiter too had originally been associated with agriculture, but then became the leading protector of Rome the City and Rome the Empire, and their most powerful god. His very name is associated etymologically with the Greek Zeus, and several of the latter's adventures were

attributed to him – inasmuch as the Roman gods were permitted adventures.

As Jupiter was lord of the sky, the sky's attributes were of course his own: he dispensed thunder and lightning, and had three thunderbolts at his disposal. Two of these were simply warnings, but the third (only to be hurled earthwards after a celestial conference) was the ultimate weapon of destruction. At his altar on the Aventine Hill, the chief magistrates of the city made sacrifices to him, for he was the symbol of man's honesty, his smaller altars being used to solemnize oaths. He seems to have been a somewhat touchy god, and easily displeased, for his priest was subject to an enormous number of strange prohibitions. He was forbidden to go on horseback, knot his hair or have it cut by a slave, spend more than three nights away from home or sleep in a bed whose legs were not smeared with clay. Moreover, his bed could not be slept in by anyone else, he had always to wear a little pointed cap, and was not allowed to touch or even mention female goats. His wife could not climb any ladder higher than the third rung, and on some days was prohibited from combing her hair. *Jupiter Optimus*

Maximus, 'the greatest', stood paramount in his chief temple on the Capitol, his face smeared with red paint as it had once been with the blood of Rome's enemies. Magnificent games were held in his honour in the autumn, and he was regularly consulted (through oracles in the sky – thunder, lightning, cloud formations and the flight of birds) about the most important matters.

The marriage of Jupiter and his sister Juno symbolized her association with earthly marriage – she watched over weddings, looked after wives in childbirth and cared for growing babies. She was perhaps outdone in beauty by Vesta, goddess of fire, whose cult again was said to have been started by Romulus, but was specially beloved because the geese which were her sacred symbols saved Rome by hissing a warning of attacking Gauls.

Juno kept watch over the family hearth and the preparation of everyday meals; though of course she had her specially dignified commemorations too, at a special sanctuary which only her own servants, the vestal virgins, were allowed to enter. For some rather vague reason, her vestals became the subject of the most intense and jealous discipline. The vow of chastity which they took when they entered her service at the age of six or seven (to remain in her temple for thirty years) was absolute; any girl who broke it was, in the early years, whipped to death; later, she was first whipped, then walled up alive in a tomb.

Vulcan, an ancient and original Roman god, was like Jupiter a god of the sun, and first god of the Tiber, and for a while he was even associated with Jupiter's wife Juno. He occasionally manifested himself on earth, as when a girl sitting by the fire was touched by a spark and gave birth to his son. When some years later that son founded a township, a crowd questioned his parentage, whereupon he prayed to his father, who set the crowd on fire, an event which seemed conclusive.

Saturn was a god of vines, said originally to have been King of Italy in the Golden Age. Vanquished and driven from his kingdom by Jupiter, he hid in Rome. His Greek associate was Cronus, one of the Titans defeated in battle by the Olympians. Saturn seems to have travelled to become god of the Etruscans by the eighth century BC. In Rome, he became keeper of the treasury and was particularly associated with money. He was a gloomy and preoccupied god who must have presided without

much pleasure over his extremely jolly feast, the Saturnalia, held during December, and a direct precursor of Christmas. This was a time of great celebration and enjoyment, when there was a public holiday and slaves were served by their masters.

Mercury, god of trade, was the Roman counterpart to Hermes, and his temple on the Aventine Hill was the gathering-place of tradesmen and merchants, especially in the month of May when the temple had been founded, apparently in honour of Hermes' mother Maia. Romans, wherever they were, seemed to enjoy forming Mercurial clubs, rather like the Rotarian clubs of the twentieth century – meetings of businessmen who came together for pleasure but were never averse to doing a little business at the same time. The worshippers of Mercury were never quite gentlemen: he was popular but lacked real prestige. Augustus was the only emperor to take much interest in him.

Apart from these major gods, there were minor ones such as Faunus, the Pan-like inventor of the pipes. Because he had once been deceived into

59

attempting to make love to Hercules rather than Omphale (the Queen of Lydia, and Hercules' mistress – they had, at the time, changed clothes) Faunus' priests always celebrated his rites naked, so that their sexual identity was clear. As god of fertility, Faunus was approached by sterile women who wanted to become pregnant; and he seems to have had a woman associate, Fauna, whose rites were performed by women alone, and are said to have been exceptionally indecent. Then there were Pales, goddess of flocks, Liber Pater, who made the ground fertile, Vilvanus, god of the woods, Flora, goddess of fruit-trees – and of course Venus.

The Greek gods in a subtle but persistent manner undermined the authority of the original Roman gods, who anyway were few. Janus and Saturn gave way to interlopers whose positions became more and more secure as their worshippers learned to attribute to them the powers and dignities they had in their Greek natures. Ceres, a nobody, took on the associations of Demeter, Greek goddess of grain, who had been wooed and won by Poseidon in the shape of a horse, and by Zeus himself in the form of a bull. Diana, originally the rather pallid goddess of woods and hills, became a real personality only when she was possessed by Artemis, the chaste huntress. And Neptune only became the familiar monarch we know when Poseidon lent him all his dignity.

Venus, in the first place a total nonentity whose task was to nurture Rome's kitchen gardens, gained her great reputation as goddess of love only when Aphrodite assumed her personality. Aeneas, Aphrodite's son, probably brought her cult with him when he landed in Italy to found the Roman race, though a shrine just outside Rome was a reproduction of the one on Mount Eryx in Sicily, dedicated to a highly lubricious goddess associated both with Aphrodite and the Phoenician Ishtar. There, temple prostitution had been the rule or habit; and at the Roman Venus' Erycine temple, the city's pimps and prostitutes held their holy days, late April and early May becoming a time of year when the most permissive plays and parties were held, and an invitation to an orgy was held to be socially acceptable.

Eros, Aphrodite's son, was translated into Cupid, son of Venus – the familiar winged boy with the golden arrows which shoot the fever of love into the veins of those they strike.

Disdaining to enter the Roman pantheon in disguise, like so many of his colleagues, Apollo swept in in person, summoned after an epidemic by means of the *Sibylline Books*, which contained spells for invoking the aid of foreign gods. By the second century BC the Greek gods had virtually taken over from the Roman ones, and ruled in Italy as forthrightly as they had ruled in Greece, ably assisted by one or two gods who had come from further afield. In 205, when Rome was pelted by stones falling from the air, the *Sibylline Books* were used to summon Cybele, the goddess of Phrygia, who organized the defeat of Hannibal, and was then much worshipped. The Emperor Caligula established a temple to Isis, the Egyptian goddess; and Caracalla built a second.

The handsome, perverse young Emperor Heliogabalus attempted to introduce Baal of Ephesus as supreme god of the Roman Empire; but the idea failed to catch on, despite the fact that troops had brought various minor Baal cults home from the wars. The last major cult to be introduced into Rome was that of Mithras, which had originated with the Aryans, and then became important in India and Persia, whence it was brought to Rome as late as the first century BC. The emperors Commodus and Diocletian supported Mithraism, and Mithraic temples have survived in ruins not only in Rome, but as far afield as the shores of the Danube and the Thames. Bulls were sacrificed to Mithras, and it was believed that it was through the blood of the sacrifice that the world began, grew and continued.

Theseus, a great hero of Attic legend, lifts aside a stone to find his father's sword beneath it – an anecdote not dissimilar to that of the English King Arthur and his discovery of the sword Excalibur. This is a terracotta relief of the first–second century AD

Below: A quiet domestic scene: Mercury warning Virgo to silence while Jupiter concentrates on his painting! Painting by Dosso Dossi, 1479–1542, who painted many scenes from the lives of the gods

Right: A somewhat saccharine Roman statue of Minerva, whose temple on the Aventine was a meeting-place for guilds of craftsmen, including dramatic poets and actors

Greece

The marvellously interesting legends of the Greek pantheon are so complex and contain so many characters that one can only sketch in an outline of their adventures. Their complicated family relationships contain a labyrinth of emotional and psychological conflicts, many of them extremely turbulent, and the anecdotes of their earliest years are among the most violent.

In the beginning was Chaos. Then Gaea, the earth, bore Uranus, who fathered (on his mother) a brood of children so vile that he immediately imprisoned them all in a deep pit. Not surprisingly, for they comprised the Titans, the single-headed Cyclopes, and three monsters with fifty heads and a hundred arms each, the Centimanes. Gaea, disapproving of Uranus' attitude to his children, persuaded Cronus, the youngest of the Titans, to castrate his father when he came to her bed. Cronus then liberated his brothers and sisters, who bore countless children, each apparently less attractive than the next, for they included Fraud, Incontinence, Murder, Lies and Disease. Cronus himself fathered a number of children on his sister Rhea, but in order to outflank a prophecy which said that one of his children would succeed him as supreme ruler, ate each one of them as soon as they were born.

Rhea, pregnant with Zeus, her youngest child, gave birth to him secretly, presenting Cronus with a

stone wrapped in a blanket, which he immediately swallowed. Young Zeus meantime was raised by nymphs on Mount Ida. When he grew up he set about avenging himself on his father. First, he persuaded a distant relative (all the gods were related to each other in one way or another) to give Cronus an emetic which made him vomit forth Rhea's other children – Hestia, Demeter and Hera, Hades and Poseidon. Then he attacked his father, secured his throne and banished him. With Zeus safely enthroned as King of the Immortals, the age of the Olympians had begun.

Zeus had his little local difficulties: the Titans opposed his kingship and attacked Olympus, the great mountain on the shore of the Aegean where the gods had their home. Zeus immediately liberated the Cyclopes, who became his allies, bringing with them their invaluable weapon, the thunderbolt. After a battle which shook the universe, so fierce were the clashes of arms, the Titans were subdued, bound with chains and buried in the ultimate depths of the earth.

No sooner were they vanquished than a race of giants – sprung from the blood spilt when Uranus was castrated – began to assault the slopes of Olympus, pelting the gods with lesser mountains which they had torn from the face of the earth, and piling Mount Ossa upon Mount Pelion in order to reach the base of Zeus' throne. With the help of the human and mortal hero Hercules, Zeus' immortal warriors triumphed. But now Gaea, jealous of Zeus' victories, created the monster Typhoeus, who actually routed Zeus' allies and captured the great god himself. Hermes rescued him, and Typhoeus was eventually crushed under Mount Etna.

Just as the continents were rent and drifted apart, the Ice Age came and went, and great floods altered the shape of the world; and just as volcanoes boiled and earthquakes rumbled, so in Greek mythology the world had reeled under the battles of the gods, which tore mountain-chains asunder and split the plains. But after the defeat of Typhoeus, all was well: Zeus had thoroughly established himself, and the age of peace began. Which is not to say that the gods under his command did not disturb that peace from time to time and in one way or another.

They were a colourful band, those twelve great gods and goddesses. The ichor which ran in their veins instead of blood made them immortal, but otherwise they resembled human beings, though

67

nine nights, but did produce the nine Muses). In the form of a bull he raped Demeter, who bore Persephone as a result; and finally married Hera, whom he had seduced aeons earlier, dressed as a cuckoo. She was, incidentally, his sister.

Settled with Hera, whom he made co-ruler of Olympus, Zeus nevertheless continued his affairs with goddesses, and also pursued many mortal women. A master of intrigue, he approached them in a number of disguises: as a flame he wooed the nymph Aegina, later turning her into an island on which he became a rock; he came to Antiope as a satyr; and to Callisto as Apollo's sister Artemis. Io he approached disguised as a cloud. Hera recognized him, and to distract her Zeus turned Io into a white heifer. Hera sent a gad-fly to torment her, and she fled across the world to Egypt, where Zeus restored her to human form. The manner in which he did this resulted in the birth of their son Epaphus.

Meanwhile, Zeus turned his attentions to Danae, daughter of the King of Argos, who had locked her away for fear of a prophecy that she would bear a son who would displace him. Zeus entered her cell disguised as a shower of gold (the mechanics of this remain obscure), and of their liaison Perseus was born. Europa, a young girl of Phoenicia (daughter, indeed, of its king: Zeus' eye usually seemed to light on girls of regal, or at least noble, birth), noticed an exceptionally handsome bull in the middle distance. Unwise enough to climb on its back, she was carried off across the sea to Crete. The bull was of course Zeus, in another of his famous impersonations. Europa bore him three children, all considerately adopted by the King of Crete, who later married her.

As a swan, Zeus seduced Leda, a young married woman; and another wife, Alcmene, received him enthusiastically when he came to her bed disguised as her husband Amphitryon. When the real Amphitryon came to her only a short while afterwards, she was somewhat puzzled by his insatiability. The result of the quick succession of couplings was Hercules, Zeus' son, and Iphicles, Amphitryon's child. There were numerous other mistresses, many of them one suspects invented by the inhabitants of various small towns in the neighbourhood of Olympus, eager to claim the kudos of a royal visit.

No wonder Hera, Zeus' legal wife, looked on

they were much more beautiful and on a grander scale (Ares, when measured, was found to be 200 yards tall). They spent their lives in drinking and merry-making, the smell of sacrificed beasts burned in their honour by mortals at the foot of Olympus rising to sharpen their appetites for the nectar and ambrosia which sustained them. Zeus presided, and Apollo provided entertaining music, with the help of the Muses.

Such a life might be expected to pall a little after the first few thousand years, and the gods beguiled their immortality with many exploits, Zeus not least among them. Always given to the arts of love, he married a number of times – his wives included Metis (whom he swallowed, eventually, for much the same reason Cronus swallowed his children), Themis and Mnemosyne (that marriage lasted only these machinations with a less than approving eye, though she occasionally got the better of her husband. For instance, she persuaded his young mistress Semele to insist that he should appear to her as himself, and as a result Semele was cremated by his glory. She did her best to retain his love, bathing each year in the immortal spring to renew her beauty, which indeed was such that she received many offers from lesser gods and mortals, all of which she spurned. Ixion, King of the Laphithae, invited to a dinner-party on Olympus, was unwise enough to show his infatuation, whereupon the jealous Zeus bound him to a fiery wheel which still whirls him through the sky.

Hera's patience occasionally gave out. She once swept out of Olympus in a rage, and was only persuaded to return when Zeus started going about with a beautiful dummy dressed as a goddess, which he introduced as his fiancée. Hera's jealousy led to various catastrophes – she inveterately disliked her husband's illegitimate children, and always did her best to injure them.

When Zeus swallowed his wife Metis, in order to prevent her having a possibly dangerous child, he reckoned without the strength of the life-force. Experiencing a bad headache after dinner, he invited Prometheus to attempt a cure. The latter struck his chief a smart blow with an axe, and from the split in his head out sprung Athene, the warrior goddess, in full armour and with a javelin in her hand. She was an incorrigible fighter, always off to war on someone's behalf; she helped Hercules in the trials visited upon him by Hera, aided Perseus against the Gorgons and gave Bellerophon the golden bridle with which he finally tamed the splendid horse Pegasus. She also took part in the war against the giants, single-handedly defeating Enceladus and Pallas, two of the most violent. This naturally commended her to her father.

Athene was an exception on Olympus, in that she never seemed to be much interested in sex. In fact she was so modest that when Teresias accidentally came across her while she was bathing, she struck him blind on the spot – though giving him by way of consolation the power to foretell the future. She seems to have had some maternal feelings, however, for when Hephaestus, the Olympians' blacksmith, attempted to rape her, and she escaped so nimbly that his sperm fell to the ground, she took the child who grew from it as her son, Erichthonius, and

brought him up. He later became King of Athens, and his adopted mother taught him how to tame horses so that they could be used, for the first time, to draw war-chariots. Despite her love of war, she contributed much to the comfort of humanity, inventing the potter's wheel and the flute. A marvellous weaver, she was only once defeated in that art: by Arachne, whom in revenge she turned into a spider.

Apollo, above all a god of light, was to be found in various manifestations all over Asia. He was perhaps the most beautiful of all the gods – almost every carving of him shows a young man of ideal beauty, beardless, with long hair, and almost always naked, the better to display himself. His mother, Leto, was said to have been one of Zeus' wives before his marriage to Hera. The latter jealously declined to regard either Apollo or his twin sister Artemis as

legitimate. Indeed, when she heard of Leto's pregnancy, she sent her pet serpent, the awful Python, to attack her. Fortunately, Apollo was born before Python arrived. Fed on nectar and ambrosia rather than milk, he was a sturdy and precocious child, and at four days old disposed of the Python and returned to Olympus crowned with laurel and hymned by accompanying priests.

Apollo was an expert archer (his arrows were made by the Olympian smith, Hephaestus), and successfully overcame various enemies. His father Zeus was proud of him and always welcomed him to his table. Son took after father in amorous proclivities, too, although several of his affairs turned out tragically. He had children by three immortals and by the nymph Cyrene, but his attempt to seduce and then to rape the nymph Daphne resulted in her being turned into a laurel-tree by Gaea. The mortal girl Castalia threw herself into a fountain rather than succumb to his advances.

Coronis, a daughter of Phlegyas, King of the Lapithae of Thessaly, happily slept with him and conceived a son; but just before giving birth, she married an Arcadian youth. Apollo, furiously jealous, put husband and wife to death, but turned up just in time to seize his child, Asclepius, from Coronis' body as it burned on the funeral-pyre. Apollo was bisexual and had several affairs with young men, including Cyparissus (who was turned into a cypress) and Hyacinthus. The latter evidently had great physical appeal, for his beauty had already seduced the poet Thamyris, the very first man to woo one of his own sex. Apollo loved him frantically; but when one day he was teaching him the art of throwing the discus, the west wind caught it, threw it at the youth and killed him.

Artemis, twin-sister of Apollo (who was one day younger), had accompanied him on his expedition against the Python, and shared his adeptness with weapons – she spent most of her time hunting with the gold bow and quiver she received from Zeus as a birthday present. She shared her brother's beauty, too, but not his amorous nature. She seems, on the contrary, to have been virginal to a fault, and shared with Athene a perhaps over-zealous modesty, for when the mortal hunter Actaeon came upon her and her retinue of equally virginal companions as they bathed naked in a fountain, Artemis changed him into a stag, set her pack of hounds on him and watched as they tore him to pieces. The only male

Hermaphroditus, the child of Aphrodite and Hermes, was a double-sexed being, and the hermaphrodite (this is a Roman carving of one) symbolised a sacred king deputising for the queen

she seems to have favoured was Orion, a hunter, described as the handsomest man alive. She took him hunting several times; but her brother Apollo, who knew about various sexual liberties Orion had taken with both mortals and goddesses, arranged for a scorpion to sting him to death. Artemis was not too broken-hearted, however, for by this time she had discovered that Orion had chased her virgin friends the Pleiades so vigorously that the gods had had to change them into stars to rescue them from him. She had also discovered that the Pleiades were far from virginal, three of them having accommodated Zeus, two Poseidon and one Ares, and another having married beneath her – to Sisyphus, a mere mortal.

There is no doubt that Artemis, whatever her beauty, was a touchy goddess. For one thing it was extremely unwise to forget to do her proper honour. Admetus, King of Therae, who forgot to make a sacrifice to her on the occasion of his marriage, was surprised to find his bridal bed full of poisonous snakes. And Oeneus, King of Calydon, who failed to present a sample of his earliest crop to her, had his entire family devoured by a giant bear.

Hermes, messenger of Zeus and god of travellers, was a son of the Father of the Gods – a title which was often more than symbolic – and Maia. The first thing the infant did was to sneak from his cradle and steal an entire herd of heifers from Apollo, later making his peace by inventing the first lyre (made from a tortoise-shell, an ox-hide and some sheep-gut) and presenting it to Apollo, who used it to establish himself as god of music. Hermes was generally an inventive youth. Besides the lyre and the pipes, he invented astronomy, the musical scale, the art of boxing, the discipline of gymnastics, weights and measures, the game of knuckle-bones and the cultivation of the olive-tree. He made himself generally popular with the gods – even Hera did not dislike him, and gave him suck. However, as he was grown-up enough to round up and steal a whole herd of heifers, this may have been as much a pleasure as a favour. He helped Zeus in his amatory adventures and had some of his own, becoming the lover of Aphrodite, Hecate and Persephone, as well as of a number of nymphs and several mortals. Visiting Penelope, Odysseus' wife, disguised as a goat, he fathered Pan, and had many other children.

Ares was a vindictive, short-tempered and generally disliked god, although handsome in his upright and militaristic way, and Aphrodite herself was happy to be seduced by him when bored with her husband Hephaestus. But they overdid things, and a neighbour told Hephaestus, who forged an unbreakable bronze net so thin that it could not be seen, and, ostensibly leaving on a journey, waited until Ares had climbed into Aphrodite's bed, threw it over the naked lovers and displayed them to the laughing gods – whereupon Hermes avowed that he would be delighted to take Ares' place, net or no net. Ares' main talent was for fighting, though he was occasionally defeated (once by a group of giants, who kept him imprisoned in a brazen tomb until Hermes came to his rescue). He had a number of affairs and a multitude of children, most of whom met unfortunate ends.

Hephaestus, the cuckold who turned the tables on Ares, may have been wronged, but one can scarcely blame his unfaithful wife Aphrodite too much, for he was the ugliest of the twelve chief gods of Olympus, a cripple with a disclocated hip, and the sad butt of his fellow-immortals. One can scarcely imagine that Aphrodite would have married him had she not been given to Hephaestus by Zeus; indeed, it was generally believed that the three sons she bore him were really fathered by Ares.

Thetis had rescued Hephaestus when, not long after his birth, his mother Hera had dropped him off a cliff, disgusted with his ugliness. Always interested in metalwork, he made her, when he was grown up, an extremely beautiful brooch; its beauty was recognized by Hera, and the truth came out. Hephaestus was readopted by his mother, who set him up as a blacksmith and arranged with Zeus his marriage to Aphrodite. During his time in Olympus (before he was unwise enough to quarrel with Zeus, and went over the cliff a second time) he made a marvellous collection of artefacts – Zeus' throne and sceptre, Achilles' armour, Agamemnon's sceptre, and the gold and silver dogs at the palace of Alcinous were among them. When Zeus invented woman to punish man, it was Hephaestus who was asked to make the original maquette for Pandora (for practice, he had already made a set of golden mechanical women to help him at the smithy).

Aphrodite herself, the *grande horizontale* of Olympus, had only one duty assigned her by the fates: to make love. This she did with great facility and enthusiasm, and no lack of volunteers. Originally, she was said to have risen from the sea, apparently fashioned out of the bloody spume which resulted when Cronus threw the severed phallus of his father Uranus into the waves. Her beauty was paramount and without peer, and her appearance in the neighbourhood of Olympus was greeted with modified rapture by the other goddesses. Eris, goddess of discord, stirred things to a climax by throwing down a golden apple inscribed 'For the fairest'. Hera, Athene and Aphrodite all bent to pick it up, and Zeus – presumably wanting to keep the peace as far as possible by not involving the Olympians more than necessary – insisted that their beauty should be judged by a mortal. Paris, a son of King Priam of Troy, was chosen as judge. One by one, the goddesses strode naked before him. Not content to impress him by physique alone, they all offered bribes. Hera promised to make him Lord of all Asia if he chose her; Athene offered him victory in every battle he fought; Aphrodite offered him herself, the most beautiful of human women, as his mistress. He handed Aphrodite the golden apple (she was wearing at the time the celebrated girdle which made everyone fall in love with its wearer). Paris won Helen of Troy; but the other two goddesses ensured that his country was devastated by the Greeks, and that he himself fell in battle.

Whatever her rivals said or did, Aphrodite was now supreme beauty of Olympus, and though married to Hephaestus, she seduced almost every other god with insatiable energy. Flattered by Hermes' comments when he had seen her trapped in the brazen net, she spent a night with him, and bore him a son – Hermaphroditus, a youth with women's breasts. She had two sons by Poseidon and another by Dionysus – Priapus, a boy with huge genitals (it is perhaps psychologically apt that as a gardener he always carries a pruning-knife).

Zeus presumably, as the greatest of the gods, had the power to resist Aphrodite and the girdle; but perhaps out of jealousy, made her fall desperately in love with a mortal, the Trojan Anchises, who bore her Aeneas. Eros, Aphrodite's son, was a great help to her in the organization of her various affairs. His father was said to be Hermes, or Ares, or Zeus himself, who some believed also to be Aphrodite's father. This last suggestion was disliked by most puritans, for it seemed to suggest that even incest was a proper product of sexual passion.

Poseidon, god of the waters, was one of those children Cronus swallowed at birth, and later

The gallant Perseus, son of Zeus and Danaë, battles with the sea-monster whose prey, Cassiopeia's daughter Andromeda, lies chained to a rock, a sacrifice to Poseidon. On a cliff near Joppa the marks of her chains can still be seen. Painting by Domenico Fetti (1589–1623)

vomited up at Zeus' behest. After he had fought at Zeus' side against the Titans and giants, he was rewarded by being made god of the waters – lakes and rivers as well as seas – and went off rather grumpily to construct a vast underwater palace at the bottom of the Aegean. He was not entirely contented with his regime, for he was endlessly ambitious and never ceased to argue that he should have had a more rewarding kingdom (technically he was the equal of Zeus, after all). But he was not a good disputer and lost the arguments.

After considerable dismay and argument on her own behalf, Amphitrite, a Nereid, consented to marry him, and bore him three children. But she had much to complain of, for he was another Lothario, and indeed it would be almost impossible to enumerate his affairs. Among his mistresses were Gaea, Demeter, Scylla (whom Amphitrite turned into a monster with six heads and twelve feet by putting a potion into her bath-water) and Medusa (whom he seduced in Athene's temple, with the result that Athene cursed the unfortunate girl with a headful of snakes).

Finally among the twelve chief gods of Olympus comes Hestia, goddess of household fire, much worshipped by mortals, but, though the eldest of the immortals, perhaps a trifle insignificant among her peers. After the dethronement of Cronus she was wooed by both Poseidon and Apollo, but swore to Zeus that she would remain a virgin for ever; she never took part in any war or dispute, and indeed stayed clear of amorous adventures. She invented the idea of building houses, and is a peculiarly domestic goddess.

Several important gods and goddesses never managed to make the top table, as it were, and remained minor immortals. Among these was Themis, a Titan who was one of Zeus' earlier wives, and was so wise and had such a splendid sense of justice that even Hera honoured her; Iris, a minor servant who among other tasks brought Zeus' messages down to earth in the form of a rainbow; Hebe, another servant, and goddess of youth; and Ganymede, abducted by Zeus, who was impressed by his beauty to become – though born a human – cup-bearer to the gods.

Apart from Pan (an account of whom will be found elsewhere), Zeus' son Dionysus merits a note. He had a traumatic infancy, for Hera instructed the Titans to seize him, tear him into shreds and boil

these in a cauldron. Rhea, his grandmother, brought him back to life, and in an attempt to disguise him from Hera, Zeus turned him into a ram. But he was discovered, and Hera sent him mad, to wander the earth for ever. There were accounts of him from Egypt, India and Phrygia, through which he travelled accompanied by his tutor Silenus and a band of wild satyrs and maenads, himself not the least unattractive figure among them, with his horns and crown of serpents. He was much given to wild parties, and anyone who would not join in would quite likely be sent mad. At Orchomenus the three daughters of the King declined to dance with Dionysus, who changed himself in quick succession into a lion, a bull and a panther. The girls were never the same again. Eventually, after spreading terror, and some ecstasy for those who shared his rather exotic tastes, he reached Olympus, where Hestia allowed him to take her seat with the other gods.

Below, left: An attic vase shows the sirens wheeling about the head of the naked, helpless Odysseus.
Below, right: Demeter and Persephone send the mortal Triptolemus to teach mankind the art of agriculture, providing him with gifts of corn, a plough, and a chariot. Painting by Makron on a bowl from Capua, fifth century BC
Lower page: Bacchus and a nymph. Tenth-century ivory casket

Egypt and the Middle East

Egyptian myth is populated by an enormous number of gods and goddesses, whose personalities are often obscure, but who – to judge by the carvings and paintings which have survived – seem to have been definite individuals. As far as one can gather, each of the tribes wandering through Egypt in the earliest times had its own god, which was in the first place an animal. So the oldest immortals of Egypt were animals which very gradually became humanized, but often retained their animal or bird heads. When the tribes began to settle, build towns and administer regions, the gods settled with them, inhabiting their own temples from which occasionally their images would be carried out to demonstrate their presence to the people. They married, had children, and sometimes whole families of gods were created, to add to the confusion.

Eventually major gods emerged, and slowly became common to most of the country. The stars, for instance, shone from the bright belly of the sky-goddess Nut, who arched herself on the tips of her fingers and toes above the virile frame of Geb, the earth-god. The Sun, Ra-Harakhte, ruled all Egypt, over which he flew every day as a great falcon.

Sometimes the sun was said to be merely the right eye of this gigantic bird, while the moon was the left eye.

The essential ruling god who had created the earth was differently named according to which religious system one consulted: at Hermopolis, he was Thoth; at Heliopolis, Ra; at Memphis and Busiris, Ptah or Osiris. It is Osiris about whose personality we know most, because the Greek historian Plutarch left a detailed account of him. Ra may have been more important at first; he had lived for ages within Nun, the world-ocean, and then hid in the bud of a lotus. Tiring of seclusion, he eventually burst brightly forth upon the earth and gave birth to twins, Shu and Tefnut, who were the parents of Geb and Nut. Having created the universe, and seen mankind spring from his tears, Ra rose every morning, and after his bath and breakfast rowed out in a boat to inspect his kingdom, spending an hour in each of the twelve provinces. When, after aeons of time, he grew old and apparently ineffectual, man plotted against him, and only after a furious battle in which Hathor, his daughter, played a leading role, was the resulting rebellion subdued. Ra, who had found the whole business extremely disagreeable, climbed on the back of his grandchild Nut (who turned herself into a cow for the occasion), and retired to heaven. There he lived in semi-retirement, continuing to ride daily in his boat across the sky from east to west, and returning to earth only in order to visit the wives of the Pharoahs in order to conceive their successors, who were accurately called Sons of Ra.

The elder son of Geb and Nut, and the tallest and one of the most handsome of all men, Osiris (whom the Greeks identified with Dionysus), succeeded his father as King of Egypt, taking Isis, his sister, as Queen. A gentle and civilized god, he wooed his people, and later the people of Asia and the rest of the known world, through music. Set, his younger brother, organized a plot against him, and at a banquet succeeded in persuading him to climb into a magnificently carved coffin which was then sealed and thrown into the Nile. It drifted to the Phoenician coast and became encased in the trunk of a splendid tamarisk-tree. Isis, hearing of a strange tree giving off a beautiful and pervasive perfume, rescued the coffin and returned it to Egypt. There Set once more got hold of it, cut his brother's body into fourteen parts, and scattered them. Isis indomitably collected them up again (except for the penis, which had been eaten by a crab), and invented the art of embalming to make Osiris whole again. Rather than embroil himself once more in earthly politics, he retired to Elysium to reign over the dead.

Osiris' gentleness and culture, his trials and the manner in which he survived them – indeed, survived death – made him especially beloved through the whole of his effective reign; and he was worshipped for at least three thousand years, perhaps longer than any other known divinity. His wife Isis became by far the most important goddess in Egyptian religion, and was worshipped well into the Christian era. Apuleius' *The Golden Ass* gives interesting details of her rites.

The kings of Egypt identified themselves with the avenging Horus, her son, miraculously conceived after her husband Osiris had been dismembered and his phallus devoured. Horus was brought up in seclusion, for fear of the wicked Set, and only his mother's fanatical devotion protected him from all sorts of natural misfortunes which dogged his childhood and adolescence. Set seems to have found him on at least one occasion, and did his best to rape him.

Osiris appeared to him from time to time to teach him the arts of war, and as soon as he was old enough he started an implacable war against Set, pursuing him and his followers remorselessly until the gods grew bored with the conflict and set up a tribunal to judge their case. Even Isis was weary of the conflict by then, and on one occasion actually intervened in favour of Set, whereupon Horus either raped her or cut off her head, according to which account of the legend one favours. Set argued before the tribunal, perhaps with some justice, that Horus had a somewhat equivocal parentage. But the gods came down in favour of his legitimacy, and he reigned triumphantly over Egypt, whose kings believed themselves to be living embodiments of his godhead.

Although Egyptian mythology has its share of violence, there are also some extremely attractive immortals in its pantheon: Hathor, for instance, Horus' wife and Ra's daughter. Spoken of as the great celestial cow who nourished all mankind, she has some affinity with the Greek Aphrodite; especially protective of women, she was goddess of music and the dance, and her temple was the home of much intoxication and great enjoyment. She sat

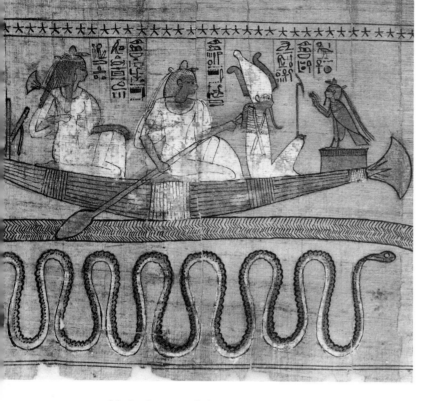

amid the leaves of the sycamore-tree on the edge of the desert to welcome the dead with bread and water before holding steady the ladder upon which they could climb to the skies, where Anubis, another god, directed them on the right road, taking them by the hand to introduce them into the presence of the Judges.

The kings of Egypt were the living personifications of Ra, just as their sons were living Horuses. But each Pharoah in addition had his own favourite gods and goddesses, the leader of whom was probably Amon, the counterpart of the Greek Zeus. Amon, whose statue often takes a phallic form, was the great god of fertility, and from the time of King Amenemhet I, of the twelfth dynasty, was god of Thebes and all Egypt.

Sometimes Amon, as Amon-Ra, absorbed the powers of his rival; sometimes Ra had a revival when the priests of Heliopolis decided to make a stand against Amon's increasing power. A new god, Aten, overcame him for a while, but Tutenkhamon ('Living Image of Amon') revived his cult, and by the time of the reign of Rameses III he had a retinue of powerful priests (one of whom succeeded to the throne), over eighty thousand servants and more than four hundred thousand head of cattle. The

ruins of his temples at Thebes, Luxor and Karnak remain to astonish us with their size and nobility.

Amon and his wife Mut had no children, but adopted two: Mont and Khons. Mont, whom the Greeks related to Apollo, had a falcon's head (or, late in his career, a bull's), and was originally Theban god of war, defeated by Amon in the contest for chieftainship of the gods. Quick of temper, Mont found it difficult to remain in the household of the King of the Gods, and left for Hermonthis, where he happily reigned as a large fish in a small pond. Amon and Mut's second adopted son, Khons, became a great healer, and the sick from far afield came to his temples to be cured. Even a prince of Syria sent his daughter to have a demon exorcized by Khons, who drove it from her in the form of a giant golden eagle.

Of the other Egyptian gods – and of many of them we know very little, for there remains no literature, their temples have crumbled and their portraits, though noble, are difficult to interpret – one or two are memorable. Sekhmet, the goddess so fearful in battle that she was represented as a lioness, is surprisingly enough the mild and gentle Hathor in disguise. When the rebellion against Ra threatened the establishment, she threw herself upon his enemies with such violence that he feared the entire human race might be exterminated. Knowing that Hathor was fond of a glass, Ra thereupon set out jugs of beer and pomegranate-juice all over the battlefield. Hathor mistook them for jugs of blood and drank so thirstily that she fell into a drunken stupor and eventually slept. She was given the name Sekhmet on that specific occasion, when the massacre ceased; and on the anniversary there was a great deal of celebration and intoxication among her admirers.

The great hero of Assyrian and Babylonian mythology is Marduk, son of Ea, Lord of the Earth and god of wisdom. Apsu, the void from which the universe had sprung, had become bored with the petty arguments of the gods, and decided on a universal cataclysm which would destroy all things and leave him in peace. To prevent this disaster, Ea took him into protective custody, but Tiamat, the goddess embodying the sea (and therefore the female principle in life) sprung to Apsu's defence, raising an enormous and terrible army of serpents, dragons and evil monsters to punish Ea's *lèse-majesté*. Backed by his father Anshar (the male principle), Ea summoned Marduk and sent him into

Left: The face of Humbaba, the demon fought by the friendly rivals Gilgamesh and Enkidu in the great epic preserved on clay tablets in the library of Assurbanipal, King of Assyria
Below: Enki, god of fresh waters, came in a golden age to Sumer to fertilise Ninhursag, Mother of the Land

battle against Tiamat and her hordes.

First insisting on recognition as supreme commander, Marduk defeated Tiamat, cut her body in two, and from it created heaven and earth, peopling the world with human beings who not unnaturally showed intense gratitude for their lives. The gods were also properly grateful, invested him with many titles, and eventually permitted themselves to be embodied in him, so that he became supreme god, plotting the whole course of known life from the paths of the planets to the daily events in the lives of men.

He remained watchful and alert, and retained his capacity for excellent generalship. There was, for instance, the case of Sin, the moon-god, who nightly rowed across the sky in his bright white boat. His nightly task of illuminating the night made him the enemy of all those wicked creatures whose doings were best concealed by darkness, and they banded together to extinguish his light. For a while they succeeded; but Marduk intervened, gained another victory, and gentle old Sin with his turban and long beard of lapis lazuli returned to his nightly journeying.

It was Sin, incidentally, who had been instructed by Marduk to mark the passing of time, which he did by altering the shape of his boat, which once a month became a full, round, shining crown. Sin was the possessor also of great wisdom, and by his wife Ningal had two sons – Shamash and Nusku – and a daughter, Ishtar. Shamash was god of the sun, who each morning appeared through the door of his house, climbed a mountain to the ledge where his coachman was harnessing his great chariot, and presently drove it up to the summit of the sky, then down to a gate leading to the bowels of the earth.

Just as Sin's pure white light distressed the evil-doers of the night, so Shamash's blazing gold light gave him the ability to discern all evil. He was Lord of Judgement, and his light shone forward so that like the Greek Apollo he could see into the future.

Nusku, Sin's third child, was god of fire, and Ishtar, his daughter, the personification of the planet Venus who rode out to the battles she fought so valiantly in a chariot drawn by seven lions. She seems not only to have been extremely pugnacious, but to have provoked quarrels even among close relatives. Ishtar was a strange being to have sprung from the peaceful planet, and her second

Above: From left to right, the warlike Ninurta, Ishtar (personification of Venus) and Ea, god of knowledge, attended by a lion, bird, fishes and a slave
Above, right: Gilgamesh and Enkidu in action
Below: A Persian monster of the Sassanian dynasty (224–729 AD)

manifestation, not as a daughter of Sin, but of Anu, son of Anshar (and therefore Ea's brother), is preferable to her first. Anu himself, though originally a supreme god, had failed to battle successfully with the renegade Tiamat, and was on the whole a peaceable character. His daughter Ishtar (in the second of her legends) took after him, and was goddess of love, though even in that manifestation she seemed to be more given to carnality than to any sprititual emotion. Bad-tempered and violent, she would visit earth in the company of a retinue of prostitutes and whores; she often threatened to make the whole of mankind impotent; and her love was so fatal that it destroyed many of her lovers.

One of these was Tammuz, god of harvest. When he died, she pursued him into the underworld, gaining entry through the seven gates by a celestial strip-tease. Naked, she reached hell, and there was imprisoned, only to be released by Asushu-Namir, a celestial hermaphrodite free of all passion.

It was among the Phoenicians that the great god Ba'al had his origin. God of storm and winter rain, his name was too sacred to be spoken; indeed, it was known only to his intimates, *Ba'al* being a pseudonym. He had fought for supremacy with the dark gods of deep waters, and emerged triumphant to become a god of virility and vegetation, constantly in combat with Mot, god of drought and sterility. Mot was eventually vanquished, though not until Ba'al himself had been killed and brought back to life by the intervention of his sister Anat.

Adonis was also a Phoenician god, an extremely handsome young man born of a tree, whose mother had assumed that form for reasons of her own. Much admired by Persephone, goddess of the underworld, he was also claimed by Aphrodite, and Zeus decided that he should spend half the year on earth and half in the underworld. He too was a vegetation god, and his festivals were among the most beautiful in the whole of Phoenician religion: they commemorated his death, and there were scenes of great and solemn mourning. Theocritus describes one celebration at Alexandria at which a statue of Adonis lay under a purple tissue, ravishing in its beauty, with Venus at its side, surrounded by silver baskets containing all kinds of plants, and vases of honey, perfumes and fruits.

The goddess the Phoenicians called Ashtart or Asherah and the Mesopotamians Ishtar, was called Astarte by the Greeks, who saw her as a counterpart of their own Aphrodite. Goddess of fertility and love, she accompanied the Phoenicians on their journeys – to Memphis and Granada, Carthage and Arabia. In Egypt she was shown naked standing on a lion, and with a lotus-flower in her hand; in Canaan (ancient Palestine) she was symbolized by an upright pole. She was said to be the wife of El, the great god who ruled all Canaan, and to have borne him seventy child-gods. The fact that she was served by hard-working prostitutes (whose incomes paid for her cult) did not commend her to the Jews, who condemned her worshippers; the Greeks disliked her effeminate priests, who dressed in women's clothing and painted their faces; and the Christians decided that she was a demon. Her cult, in its many forms, eventually vanished unmourned.

Many of the great gods of the Middle East can be found in one of the most important pieces of Assyro-Babylonian literature, the *Epic of Gilgamesh*, a magnificent poem which survived as part of the library of King Assurbanipal of Assyria. Gilgamesh's adventures, too long and complicated to summarize here, involved many deities, and resulted in his narrowly missing immortality – the secret of eternal youth was stolen from him by a serpent while he was bathing. Gilgamesh himself was, incidentally, originally a real King of Sumer.

Persia

In the great Sassanian age of Persian myth (*c.* AD 200–750) – long after the simple worship of the all-powerful god of fire, Atar, in the earliest times – the supreme gods were Ormazd and Ahriman, God and the Devil, Good and Evil. Ormazd recited the story of his creation of the world to the prophet Zoroaster (or Zarathustra), who lived seven centuries before Christ, and this is related in the Zend-Avesta, written perhaps in about AD 500. Ormazd was at first alone in the universe, but with the gift of foresight recognized Ahriman as he took cloudy shape in the dense night before creation. A fruitless debate between them lasted for three thousand years. Another three thousand, Ormazd foresaw, would enable him and Ahriman to collect themselves and create human beings to be used as gun-fodder in the battle to come; a third three thousand years would consist of a shuttlecock and battledore game between good and evil; and in the final three thousand years before the end of the world, Ormazd would finally emerge as overall victor.

Ormazd had under his control six major immortals: Bahman, the Good Spirit; Arbidihist, the Righteous Spirit; Shahriver, the Spirit of Dominion; Sipendarmith, Spirit of Piety; Khordadh, Spirit of Perfection; and Mourdad, Spirit of Immortality – beings not dissimilar to the archangels of Christianity. They worked in various areas of life: Bahman looked after working animals, Arbidihist kept fires alight, Shahriver governed the movements of the planets and stars, and the three remaining spirits ruled earth, water and vegetation.

Below these spirits came the equivalent, roughly, of the angels: the Yazatas, of whom Ormazd himself was the first, and Zoroaster a worldly example. Ahriman had his servants too – the Daevas, whose life was a constant fight against goodness. They inhabited Ahriman's uncomfortable domain, where it was icy winter for ten months of the year (for 'cold is the root of all evil'). The Daevas often seem to have 'marked' the immortals like tenacious football forwards: Bahman was continually aware of the lurking presence of Ako-Mano, lying in wait for men he could deceive and then tip into the bottomless pit of immorality. Sauru marked Shahriver, undermining his divine authority. Naosihaithya watched Sipendarmith, encouraging atheism – and so on. Aeshma, who combated Sraosha the good Spirit of Obedience, perhaps deserves mention: he found his way, as Asmodeus,

into the Book of Tobit in the Apocrypha.

Ahriman's minor servants were roughly the equivalent of witches: Drujs and Pairikas were both always female – the first invariably hideous, the second capable of assuming the most beautiful and erotic forms. One of the Drujs was Jahi; polluted by a kiss from Ahriman, her impurity burst forth as menstruation, previously unknown to women. The Druj Nasu had the unpleasant habit of turning herself into a fly to feed on corpses.

The spirits of good and evil, and in particular various Drujs and Pairikas, winged their way in and out of the myths of Persia, with the earthly heroes encouraged or beset by them. The first man, Gayomart, and his children Mashya and Mashyoi, were corrupted by Ahriman, as Adam and Eve were by the Devil. Sometimes good prevailed, sometimes evil: Tahmuras the King managed to saddle Ahriman like a manic horse, and ride him over the face of the world, then forced captive demons to

teach him to write. Jam the King was saved by Ormazd from the flood, but then was beset by pride, captured by Zohak (a king's son possessed by Ahriman) and sawn in two. Zohak was taught to eat flesh (repugnant to naturally vegetarian man), and became himself a formidable demon. He ruled for a period of absolute terror before being defeated by the good Feridun, who ruled for five hundred years in a regime as good as Zohak's had been evil. The love of Zal, a great hero, for the fabulously beautiful Rudabeh is a magnificent romance; their son Rustem prevailed against many demons.

In Moslem Persia there was a horde of gods before the triumph of Islam; almost fifty of them, each important in a particular sphere. The cult of astrology produced personalized gods too, in the planets: the Sun as the protector of kings, Saturn as the friend of crooks and Venus the Madame of prostitutes, Mercury patron of writers, Mars of soldiers, and Jupiter of priests and religious men.

India

Aryan invaders who conquered northern India before the second millennium BC brought to the simple natives of the Punjab area their own religion headed by the god Dyaus, an equivalent of Zeus. The Brahmans, or priests, inherited the Vedic literature and its myths, the most notable god of which was Indra. In human shape (the only one of the gods in the Vedas shaped like an earth-being) Indra was a warrior-god, armed with a thunderbolt and riding in his chariot, the sun. In this splendid vehicle – impressive in India to an extent unknown in colder northern climes – he broke the clouds to bring rain and nurture the crops.

He had a rival in his power: the three-headed son of Tvashtri, who disliked him. When the boy showed signs of being indeed worthy of the highest office, Indra killed him; and in revenge Tvashtri (a Brahman with magical powers) spawned a demon, Vritra, so immense that he swallowed Indra in one furious gulp. Mistaken enough to open his mouth, Vritra lost the god, but Indra was forced to trick out a peace with the demon on condition that the latter would never be destroyed either by day or by night, or with a weapon of wood, stone or iron, or anything wet or dry. One evening just as day was giving way to night, Indra made a weapon of sea-spume, and struck Vritra dead with it.

Mitra and Varuna, colleagues of Indra, have no

Left: Siva, Lord and Master, is worshipped as the principle of generation, and (as here) his head is often carved as part of a lingam or phallus
Centre: Vishnu and Lakshmi, his wife, ride serenely on his great eagle, Garuda, greeted by earthly kings
Right: The entirely delightful elephant-headed god Ganesa, friendly deity of riches and success

recognizable shape: they took the form of sun and moon, respectively, so that they could be seen by man as they presided over universal law and order. Varuna was in control of both physical events and moral ideas, regulating and categorizing them. Mitra's task is less easy to define, but the two gods together are known as Rajas, or kings.

The second pair of gods to watch over man were identified with the morning and evening stars. The Nasatya were the healers, who cared for the health of the other gods, and also presided over love and marriage (they were equated with the Greek Dioscuri, Castor and Pollux). They were the children of the Sun and of Saranya, a cloud-goddess – not particularly nobly born, and indeed even refused entry into heaven because of their lower-class origin until Syavana, a wealthy man to whom they had given the gift of eternal youth, pleaded with Indra and gained entry for them.

Hindu myth was presided over by two great gods: Rudra, who later became Siva, and Vishnu. Rudra was a great archer, his arrows fatal to man and beast alike. From his vantage-point on top of the highest mountains he was able to choose his victims with unerring accuracy, terrifying his fellow-gods as well as man. He became Lord of all Animals as a result of a contretemps with Prajapati, the master of created beings. He happened to see Prajapati making love to

his own daughter, Ushas, and was offered power over the animals on condition he did not execute Prajapati for incest. He agreed, but the execution nevertheless took place.

Rudra gradually became Siva because of just that sort of behaviour: he was so vicious, dangerous, uncompromising and untrustworthy that he was called Siva the Benevolent on the off-chance that that might conceivably flatter him into behaving in a more civilized fashion. It did not. With his necklace of skulls and surrounded with a retinue of fearful demons, he remained formidably unpleasant, perhaps the least attractive, most ungiving of all gods. The leader of demons and vampires, he had four arms and three eyes; he wore a tiger-skin with a snake about his neck and others about his arms – the skin lifted by a finger-nail from the back of the animal sent to destroy him by a band of heretics, the snakes tamed when they were sent against him for the same purpose. His terrible beauty attracted his worshippers to him: and indeed while he destroyed, he was also merciful. Life to him was a great game, into which man should enter with the joy and freedom of a dance. It was as a splendid dancer that he was able to reassure and convert ten thousand sceptics. He had his moments of apparent altruism. Once, when a great snake spewed out poison which threatened to destroy the world, it was Siva who drank it all down. He was an equivocal being: perhaps one of the more truthful incarnations of the human spirit in god form, for he saw both good and evil with great clarity, representing the harshness of human consciousness as well as its ecstasy.

Vishnu was an amalgam of a number of gods. His skin was dark blue, and dressed in yellow he rode an eagle, grasping in his four arms a mace, a sea-shell, a disc and a lotus-flower; or he lounged at home in Vaikuntha in a palace of gems, on a bed of lotus-flowers, his beautiful wife Lakshmi at his side.

From time to time, Vishnu is incarnate on earth: his most famous and happiest visit was as Krishna, born at Mathura between Delhi and Agra, to Devaki, a sister of King Kamsa. Like so many gods of Olympus, he narrowly escaped destruction at birth, for it had been predicted that one of Devaki's children would assassinate the King. So Vishnu grew up secretly amid shepherds, and early in his life became famous for his strength, temporal as well as spiritual, fighting demons and defeating a water-snake. The shepherdesses were unanimously in favour of him. He took advantage of this by stealing

their clothes when they were bathing, and insisting that they reclaim them by coming up to him naked, their hands folded in prayer, to make personal application. They showed little reluctance. So many girls fell in love with him, indeed, that they could not all hold his hand when he danced with them: so he divided himself up into enough Krishnas to go round.

There is to this day great rivalry between Vishnu and Siva: followers of each regard him as the true god. At the end of each creation – and they come in cycles of thousands of millions of centuries – Vishnu sinks quietly to sleep on his carpet of lotus-flowers. When he wakes, a lotus grows out of his navel, and in the middle of the flower sits Brahma, the god of creation, holding the Vedas in his four hands. Brahma then creates the next universe, while Siva emerges from his forehead, ready again to compete for its destruction.

Brahma, incidentally, made the first woman,

Sarasvati, and married her. She is goddess of music, wisdom and knowledge.

Buddhism replaced the Vedic tradition when it sprang up in the region of the Himalayas and the Ganges in about the seventh century BC. Buddha was miraculously conceived by Queen Maya, who in a dream saw a bright, beautiful, tiny white elephant enter her womb. As soon as the newly born Buddha's foot touched the earth, a lotus-flower grew beneath it, and he took possession of the world. As a young man he had a vivid delight in the arts and human sexuality, but later became an ascetic. Leaving the beautiful wife to whom he had been married, he rode out into the night on his fine horse Kantaka, cut off his hair, gave away his clothes and entered a Brahman hermitage. After a great battle with Mara, a Buddhist demon, he preached his gospel at Benares, and for forty-four years went about the land continuing to preach and to perform miracles. At the age of eighty he died, apparently of indigestion.

China

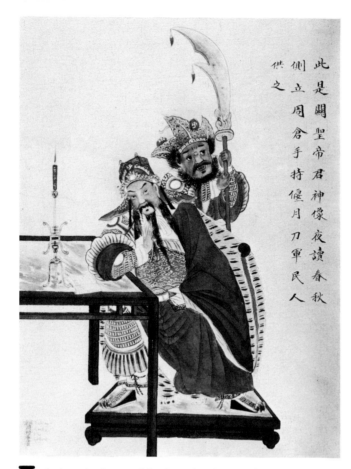

此是關聖帝君神像夜讀春秋
側立周倉手持偃月刀軍民人
供之

It is ironical, considering the form of government under which China at present finds itself, that the August Personage of Jade, who for centuries presided over the pantheon of Chinese gods, was really at the head of a complex and extremely efficient bureaucracy. This conception of the immortal hierarchy was encouraged by the emperors of China, for their own purposes.

As is the case in most immortal families, the earliest recognized presiding god was neither the first supernatural being nor necessarily in a permanent position of power. The Heavenly Master of the First Origin preceded the August Personage, and waiting in the wings was the Heavenly Master of the Dawn of Jade of the Golden Door, eventually to succeed him at the head of the company of immortal civil servants. But in recorded history, the August Personage (sometimes called the August Supreme Emperor of Jade, sometimes Father-Heaven) reigned supreme from his head office in a huge palace.

He ran his court just as an earthly ruler: he had various heads of departments, and could command an army to fight evil spirits. It was he who made man out of clay, and set the thousands of tiny maquettes out in the sun to dry. Unfortunately, rain fell, and some of them were damaged: these were the sick or deformed people of the world.

He had a family life. His wife, the Queen Mother Wang, was hostess at the banquets at which guests ate the fruit of immortality which grows once every three thousand years on the peace-trees in the imperial orchard.

Sun, Moon, Rain, Thunder and Wind were also gods; perhaps the most effective and most feared was My Lord Thunder, who punished the evildoers of earth – who are often guilty of secret crimes their neighbours know nothing about. A man struck by a thunderbolt is undoubtedly being punished for some perhaps secret enormity. Superior to him and his colleagues were the Dragon-Kings, four gods who shared out quantities of rain to given regions of the country. They lived in separate palaces, and had an army of crabs, crayfish and ordinary fish at their disposal. There were a large number of minor Dragon-Kings, one presiding over almost every separate well or stream.

Wen Ch'ang was an important and experienced personage. After he had lived through seventeen lives, he was considered sufficiently practised to be invested with the title of god of literature; he and his assistant K'uei-hsing, god of examinations, presided over the hopes of students, especially at examination time. K'uei-hsing shared with My Lord Thunder a quite excessive ugliness.

There were several perhaps more approachable gods than the last two: Shou-hsing, for instance, the god of long life, represented by the star Canopus. He carried in one hand the peach of immortality, and generally was attended by a stork or a turtle, symbolizing longevity. He decided the dates of everyone's death, writing them on a tablet (though occasionally he could be persuaded to juggle with the figures, turning 18 upside-down to read 81, for example).

Fu-hsing and Lu-hsing, gods of happiness and salaries, were originally real men, but became divinities after their deaths.

The August Personage delegated the special care of men to the Great Emperor of the Eastern Peak, T'ai-yueh-ta-ti. He arranged the whole course of the life of every man, and indeed of every animal, with

Opposite: Kuan-ti, god of war (opponent of Confucius, god of literature); famous for prediction. *The Romance of the Three Kingdoms* tells his story. As this nineteenth-century screen painting shows, he had two faces: the face of war was only assumed reluctantly, for his main task was to prevent conflict rather than encourage it
Right, below: Shou-hsing, god of long life, holding the peach of immortality: a carving of the Ming dynasty

the help of a galaxy of civil servants working in over eighty offices to determine the extent of men's riches, marital happiness, number of children, social status. His daughter, the Princess of Streaked Clouds, cared for women and children and attended births.

The staff of the Great Emperor's eighty offices was drawn from the souls of the dead; and somewhat similarly the gods of walls and ditches were also human beings who became immortal because of the goodness or value of their lives on earth. Each district had one of these gods, to police the public places. The gods of China indeed seemed to come more closely into connection with the people than the gods of many other civilizations. The hearth-god Tsao-wang, for instance, kept a careful record of the actions and words of every member of a family, and made a personal report to the August Personage, who on that evidence decided what amount of happiness or sorrow should be allotted to that family during the coming year. The Door Gods, Men-shen, kept away evil spirits from the house where they were set on guard, and the humblest hut could invite their protection as surely as the richest mansion.

There were other popular gods to whom it was possible, indeed desirable, to address oneself: Ts'ai-shen, god of money, for example, who also had his own government department to look after various aspects of the distribution of wealth. The Emperor Kuan-ti predicted the future; then there were eight immortals who seemed sometimes to serve no distinct purpose, but wandered about in a generally friendly fashion, and were as of right present at Lady Wang's banquets. They included Chang Kuo-lao, an old gentleman who travelled for many thousand leagues a day on a donkey which, when unwanted, was folded up like a piece of paper, and Lu Tung-pin, who was permitted to reward virtue and punish sin, on the spot.

Then there were separate gods for almost every profession; sea-gods and country-gods; and there were the gods of hell – or of eighteen hells, each set aside for sinners of a particular type, and ruled by the Kings of the Ten Law-Courts, each of which had jurisdiction over those who committed specific crimes. The Chinese hells were no less unpleasant than hells of any other religion; but there was the advantage at least of a sort of visiting magistrate or Ombudsman, Ti-tsang Wang-p'u-sa, who could mitigate punishment.

Right: A river spirit – the Mistress of the Hsiang River –
serenely walking on the water
Below: Chinese Taoist spirits, normally hiding in the woods,
prepare to present themselves in human form to the Buddha.
From a painting by Li Kung-lin

Overleaf, top, and below: A miscellany of Japanese spirits
Opposite: Ariadne and Dionysus, perhaps at their wedding.
A Roman mosaic from North Africa

Japan

The many gods of Japan can be traced back to the brother and sister Izanagi and Izanami, the youngest couple of seven generations of gods. They stirred up the waters of the earth and created an island on which they came together so that Izanami gave birth to the islands of Japan, and to many gods. The god of fire during his birth caused his mother so much agony that she died; Izanagi followed her into hell and rescued her; but they parted, and of each were born in various curious ways still more gods.

From the left eye of Izanagi, for instance, was born Amaterasu, goddess of the sun, from his right eye Tsuki-Yomi, god of the moon, and from his nose Susanoo, god of the seas – a fertility god of thunder, storm and rains, capable both of good and evil deeds. He was the father of O-Kuni-Nushi, god of healing, who fell in love with his sister Suseri-Hime, and underwent many trials before love triumphed.

The various loves and marriages of these earliest gods eventually culminated in the famous Jimmu-Tenno, grandson of the sea-god, who was the ancestor of the imperial family of Japan, a direct forbear of the emperors. From his reign the official history of Japan began.

There were so many rank-and-file gods that a list would be virtually endless – the early texts speak of eight hundred myriads of them, and it is true that every region, town, village and even the poorest inhabitant had a personal god and his servants. Even a stone with an unusual shape would be recognized as a Kami: and while a Kami, a venerable spirit, did not precisely represent the Western idea of a god, the principle was not dissimilar.

Amaterasu reigned as supreme goddess under the advice of a committee of other gods: her sister, Wakahiru-Me; Hiruko, god of the morning sun; Tsuki-Yomi, god of the moon; and others. Then there were storm- and thunder-gods, gods of the sea, fire, earthquake, the hearth, rice, stones, rivers. . . . And when Buddhism came to Japan in about 522, and was eventually made the official religion, other deities became popular – a great many of them being led perhaps by Amida, who vowed never to enter Nirvana until he had saved all mankind, and by Kannon Bosatu, a Bodhisattva of infinite mercy worshipped by all Buddhist sects.

Emma-Hoo, a notorious demon, ruled over Jigoku, or hell, helped in the process of judging evil men by eighteen generals and eighty thousand men.

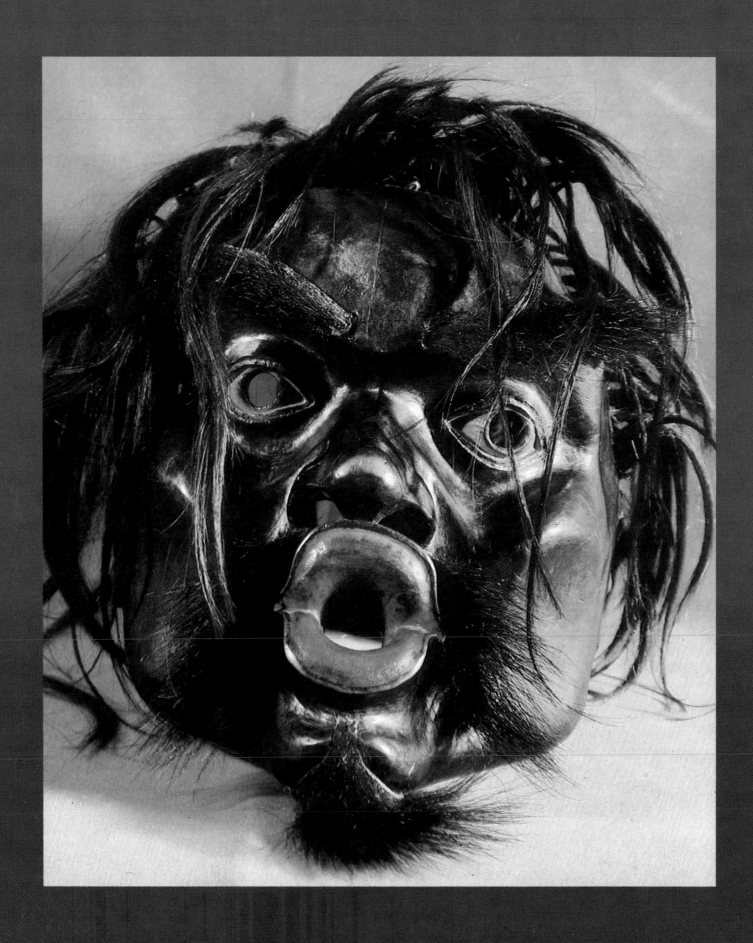

Opposite: Tsonoqua, cannibal giant of the Kwakiutl Forests of
N.W. America
Below: Choki, an irate Japanese warrior, deals with an
intransigent demon

Australasia

Out of the earth, or from the sea, came the mythical being – called Biral or Bundjil, Nurundere or Baiame – who created the aborigines of Australia. Sometimes he fathered recognizable heroes who were themselves immortal, like the dingoes of western Australia, two aristocratic wild dogs that became human giants which surveyed the land, drew water from the earth by thrusting pointed sticks into it at intervals, named all plants and animals, and eventually became high clouds in the clear skies.

It is in The Dreaming (a self-explanatory state which surely also saw the birth of many world myths) that the aborigines discovered their immortals, many of whom took the form of humans. To Arnhem Land came the two Djanggawul sisters from the island of the dead – daughters both of the Sun and the Morning Star, which respectively warmed and guided them on their long sea journey. There was a well-worn cult of Kunapipi, who mothered a vast number of children as she travelled about the country.

There are charming, poetic legends – of the origin of fire, for instance: an emu's egg, thrown into the air, set fire to a pile of sticks and became the sun. The Aruntas of central Australia, on the other hand, believed that the Sun was an old woman who climbed laboriously into the heavens each morning, and tottered down again each evening. The Narrinyeri of south Australia agreed that the Sun was an old woman (dressed in a red kangaroo-skin), but believed that she went every night to visit the land of the dead.

The aboriginal myths are simple, however; not for them the great complex pantheons of immortals in lands beyond the grave. They invented gods, on the whole, to explain the physical aspects of life, the shapes of hills, the presence of springs or deserts. The Maoris of New Zealand are a different matter. A thousand years ago they reached New Zealand from Polynesia, bringing with them the flavour of the infinitely rich mythology of Oceana. Some Maoris believed that earth and heaven had always existed; others that they were created by Io, a god of whom very little was known. Tangaroa also helped in the creation of the world, and protected humans who wore his talisman. Other Maoris believed in a kind of family-tree of gods: Rangi, the sky, was the son of Huge Light, a child of Damp, a daughter of No-parents – and the line could be traced back

through Wobbly, Unpleasant and Enduring Light to Daylight, Light, and an apparent ur-god, Po. The layman was far more familiar, however, with other gods who were the children of Rangi and Papa, the sky and the earth. Before time was, Rangi had fallen in love with Papa, fell upon her and embraced her with such violence that everything else in creation was crushed and stifled. Their children, led by Tane, were forced to pry their mother and father apart so that creation could breathe. Tane then tailored a cloak to cover his father's nakedness: the gems with which it is decorated can be seen shining in the sky on a dark night.

The gods of woods and fields, war and peace, were left pretty much to themselves: it was considered impertinent to trouble them except in cases of real emergency. The god of war, for instance, would be consulted only before a major battle; mere skirmishes were the responsibility of the earthly chiefs.

Some of the gods appeared on earth in the form of animals: sea-snakes and crabs, snakes and eels. Some of them were monstrous and horrible – hairy men, for example, who when examined were found to be made of gnarled wood. Some never showed their faces, but were nevertheless alive and dangerous – like Ngahue, the thunder-god, or Hine-nui-ta-po, both of whom were believed to guard and administer the underworld, or underworlds, for some Maoris believed there were ten. Two other gods, Rohe and Miru, assisted by looking after the less hellish districts of the land of the wicked dead.

Oceania

In common with those of other civilizations, the most important gods of the Pacific Islands were those responsible for the creation of the world and of mankind – the ones who existed before man, and will exist after him. But having said that, any attempt to discuss the Oceanic gods as though they lived in a carefully ordered, hierarchic pantheon, as neat and universal as that of the gods of Greece, becomes fruitless. An enormous crowd of rather amorphous immortals throngs the mythology of New Guinea, Fiji, Polynesia, New Caledonia, Samoa, Hawaii. Part of the problem is, of course, that most of the Oceanic civilizations have no 'literature' as we understand it. Stories of the gods have come down by word of mouth, treated with respect but not with any strict regard for accuracy in repetition. The narratives twine about each other, the same gods appear under different names, or different gods under almost the same name. Sometimes within quite a small compass two civilizations will have evolved quite different myths; or a myth will seem to have travelled hundreds of miles more or less intact.

The name of the original creator, for instance, is Konori in New Guinea, Ngendei (who hatched man out of a celestial egg) in Fiji, Tamakaia and Maui-Tikitiki in the New Hebrides, Tui (a goddess) in Samoa. . . . Some of the creation myths are very simple. On the small island of Nauru, however, there is an extremely elaborate account of the goddess Old Spider, who created the world inside a vast clam which she had found, made the sun and moon out of two snails, and the sea from the sweat of a vast worm. The top half of the clam became the vault of the sky, and the bottom half the earth. Ta'aroa, the creator god of the Society Islands, of which Tahiti is one, at first existed in the Stygian darkness of the inside of an egg, until presumably boredom drove him to invent the islands and the sea around them.

Sun and Moon are quite often the eldest children of the creator-god, or of the first men. In Queensland, the Sun (who is female) was made by the Moon (an unusual reversal of the more usual procedure): she has two legs, but an enormous number of arms, which may be seen if one looks (dangerously) directly at her. In the legends of the Gilbert Islands, when Na Reau had created the first men and women, he made them innocent of sexuality. But, like Adam and Eve, they fell, and had three children – the Sun, the Moon and the Sea (the latter, with its pervasive influence on the lives of the

islanders of Oceania, is as often specially the subject of a creation myth as the earth is to continental peoples).

The creation of mankind is often accounted for in a simple way: usually, by the chance, often unexplained, meeting of a single man and woman. Or it may simply be stated that the first couple was made by some unknown power, out of rushes (at Luzon in the Philippines), stones (at Celebes in the Dutch East Indies), trees (in Admiralty Island) or – most usually – clay. Then life was breathed into the models, in some way or another – the aborigines of Encounter Bay in south Australia believed that the creator made models from excrement, then tickled them to make them laugh, and thus brought them to life.

Only relatively rarely is the creating god or goddess given a distinct personality. The fact that man was made by *a* god is stated by, for instance, the islanders of Kei Islands, some islands in New Guinea, and in Hawaii. In the Central Carolines, a goddess is believed to have come down to earth and become mysteriously pregnant, while the Kayan of Borneo believed that man was born from a heavenly

tree embraced by a vine. Sometimes, man was born of a male god, and woman of a goddess. In Banks Islands, myth has it that man was moulded in clay and woman made of basketwork; in Queensland, that man was carved in stone and woman in boxwood.

The people of the Banks Islands to the north of the New Hebrides told how their god Quat originally made men and pigs equal: but men soon became more equal than pigs, and the latter were forced to go down on all fours so that the difference could more clearly be seen. It was Quat who found eternal daylight so tiring to the eyes that he set out to buy darkness from Night, in exchange for a pig. He returned to his domain complete with a generous supply of darkness, and a rooster. When man saw the sun disappearing for the first time, he was extremely frightened; but Quat taught him sleep, and when he considered that his creation had been idle long enough, snipped the night short with a piece of sharp stone, and set the rooster off as a natural alarm-clock.

Tane, the son of Rangi and Papa (sky and earth) in Maori legend, is found also in the myths of Hawaii, Cook Island, and the Society Islands, where he was especially concerned with everything made of wood (the stone axe was his symbol).

The great gods of Oceania somewhat lack personality, perhaps because they remained distant and impersonal beings even to those who invented them. It was impertinent of man to approach them, and there were minor gods whose job it was to look after everyday life and its problems. Perhaps, too, it is true that the men who invented them were less sophisticated than men elsewhere, who had a wider range of experience. Take, for example, the American Indians, who were less tied to a restricted environment.

One god who escaped those restrictions to become something of a character was Rongo, of Polynesia (in Hawaii he was Lono, and in the Marquesas Islands, Ono). He was god of all growing things, and his festivals celebrated or invoked plentiful harvests. He sailed away from Hawaii after the death of his wife, but promised to come back soon with a canoeful of food. When Captain Cook landed, he was mistaken for Lono, and the islanders' disappointment ended in Cook's murder.

The myths of the Pacific Islands have by now been very thoroughly studied. They are individual and characteristic, and, while they contain few mysteries (apart from practical problems such as the means used on Easter Island to raise the immense stone statues which were a part of their ancestor-worship), one of the strange facts about them is the absence of really vivid characterization in their heterogeneous pantheon. It is as though the corporate imagination of a great mass of people is needed to invent a real family of gods. The population of Oceania may simply have been too scattered, too thinly dotted about the largest body of water on the earth's surface, to make it possible for the various imaginative myths to coagulate into a body of vivid and lively legend peopled by recognizable immortals.

An eagle of the Kwakiutl tribe in the
Pacific North West: several of their many
creation myths involve birds

The Americas

The only truly indigenous mythology of the United States of America – indeed, of the Americas as a whole – is that of the American Indians. The 350 tribal groups and their numerous sub-divisions in North America alone have the most fascinating and complex mythological history. Wherever the Indians came from – and arguments as to their Mediterranean, Australasian or Asiatic origins still persist – their myths are peculiarly their own, having no obvious connection with European or Eastern mythology. Many of them centre upon the animals which were, for the hunter, the most important immortals he could conceive. Animals had inhabited earth before man. Like the cave-man of Europe whose drawings on the rough walls of his cell immortalized the creatures which, with their claws and wings, were a great deal better equipped physically to fend for themselves than he was in his weaponless, toolless state, the Indian came to regard animals as sharing his own spirit: as being at once animal *and* man. Almost every animal has been given godhood by one tribe or another, and even the bat appears immortal in Aztec art.

When man arrived on the scene, the animals left their comfortable, open homelands to take refuge in woods and streams and lakes. As they had the ability to take on the shape of man if a hunter ever happened to stumble upon an animal village, he would find the animals relaxing in recognizably human forms. If he could persuade them to accept him, he would learn from them many of the magic secrets of life. It might be thought that the hunter's necessity to kill for food would have disposed of the romantic idea of immortal animals. But he surmounted this by asserting that no animal ever really died – as long as all the bones were preserved, together with any part of the body that was not devoured by the hunter, the animal would simply reconstitute its body. If a single bone was lost, however, there would be trouble for the hunter and animal concerned: a hunter who lost a single salmon's bone made the Salmon Boy lame for life.

Each species of immortal animals was led by one single animal larger than the rest: an Owner or Elder Brother who was sometimes a spirit animal which could not be caught, and sometimes a 'real' one, recognizable by some physical quirk. The Salish of the north-west coast knew the Salmon Elder Brother by the twist of his mouth, and if caught he had to be cooked and eaten with special ceremony.

An Elder Brother watches hunters with particular care, eager to ensure that not one bone of his prey is lost hazarding the difficult business of resurrection. He is so powerful that he can quite simply make it impossible for any hunter to catch anything. A careless man who loses a bone, or worse, throws the bones of a dead quarry to his dogs, will find that the game disappears from his hunting grounds, leaving him to starve. The spirit of any animal maltreated by a hunter (that is, not cleanly killed for food or some other acceptable purpose) complains to his Elder Brother who, if the complaint is justified, will keep the spirit by him, instead of issuing it to the body of a new caribou or moose or wolf. Man, too, has his Elder Brother, called by different names – Great Being, Our Owner or Our Creator – but his duties are rather vague. Only the bear has no Elder Brother; bears are sufficient unto themselves.

One of the most notable and legendary of all Elder Brothers is Big Rabbit or Mänäbusch, who originated in Wisconsin, and became a sort of folk-hero to the mid-west Algonquin. Big Rabbit is really an enormous hare, and men and women are his uncles and aunts, to whom he taught handicrafts, and for whom he vanquished the monsters of the deep and rebuilt the world after the Flood. He was once swallowed by Meshekenabec, the great lake-serpent with many-coloured scales, but cut his way out of its belly. Big Rabbit's eternal battle with the water-monsters began when they drowned his young brother Wolf, and thus invented death. Wolf rules over the dead now, in a beautiful and happy land where the evil are not allowed, but are plunged into a fast-running river from an insecure bridge over which the good safely pass. In his attempts to revenge Wolf, Big Rabbit killed a number of water-monsters before they caused the Great Flood and a fearful winter. He still survives, and is celebrated in many ways.

The Iroquois have a pantheon of Elder Brothers who hunt in heavenly pastures during the day, retiring each evening to the dark side of the sky below the horizon: Dappled Fawn and Red Meteor, Wind Who Moves About from Place to Place, Fire Dragon with a Body of Pure White Colour, Otter, Wolf, Duck, and Aurora Borealis, among others. They originated in years long past when a beautiful girl, Awenhai, offered her hand in marriage to the celestial Chief, who lived beneath the Onodja-Tree

Opposite, left: Mictlantecuhtli, Lord of the Dead among the Totonac of Mexico.
Left, above: Quetzalcoatl, Mexican god of wind, Master of Light.
Left, below: Xipe-Totec, a god dressed in the skin of a sacrificed man, during an agricultural festival

Below: Xochiquetzal, goddess of flowering plants: the ornament in her nose indicates her rank

whose blossom lit up the world. The Chief made her pregnant by a single exhalation of his breath – apparently without knowing it, for when she began to swell with child, he became jealous of Aurora Borealis, and of Fire Dragon with a Body of Pure White Colour (both of whom he evidently suspected of misconduct). He uprooted the Onodja-Tree and, through the hole in the canopy of heaven made by its roots, pushed the Elder Brothers (though their ghosts remained with him in heaven) and his wife.

Awenhai fell towards a vast sea. Great Turtle surfaced in time to catch her, and Muskrat brought up sufficient mud from the sea-bed to make a land on which she could live. On this land, which quickly was covered by plants and trees, Awenhai lived and gave birth to a daughter, who in turn was made pregnant by an arrow carelessly (or perhaps purposely) left at her bedside by a handsome but anonymous suitor. Two children were conceived. They began quarrelling even before they left the womb, one emerging unkindly through her armpit, thus killing her. This was Oterongtongnia. His brother, Tawiskaron, born in the normal way, was literally a Man of Flint.

Awenhai, displeased at her daughter's death, threw Oterongtongnia out, and placed the body of the dead girl on a tree (it became the sun), and her head in the branches of another tree (to become the moon). Oterongtongnia, to occupy his idle time, made the earth and all the good and beautiful things in it. Tawiskaron, jealous, did his best to obstruct his brother and was able to spoil several perfectly good projects before Oterongtongnia managed to frighten him off by building an immense fire and then pursuing him with such fury that he shattered to pieces and became the Rocky Mountains. The adventures of the brothers are still enthusiastically told and play a part in the religion of the Iroquois who live in south-west Ontario, on the upper Allegheny, and near Syracuse.

The Kwakiutl have a charming story about the origin of the world. When only animals inhabited earth, and lived in two villages, one headed by Raven and Otter and the other by Head Wolf, rivalry boiled over, which resulted in Raven and Otter attacking and destroying Head Wolf's village. But this was perhaps fortunate, for they immediately began creating the world as we know it, and raising crops to feed newly made man, who at first was invented as an alternative form of food for animals.

The broad skies and open lands of the plains concentrated the attention of the tribes who lived there on the two major elements of their life – earth and sky – and their presiding immortal was the Great Spirit or Master of Life, sometimes simply called the Great Mystery. With the Sioux he was Wakonda, and with the Pawnees, Tirawa the Arch of Heaven, and he ruled with the aid of other gods – the Sun, the Moon, the Earth, the Morning Star, Wind, Thunder and Fire.

Animals might make limited excursions into the world of men, disguised in human flesh, but man lacked the power to transform himself. Animal was basically spirit; man, flesh and blood. But this is not to say that man was never deified: Huitzilopochtli, for instance, an early Aztec warrior chief, actually became the Sun. In order to keep him in the sky he had to be invigorated by human sacrifice. The victims themselves, painted white, were destined to become stars, and so at least were confident of immortality – which cannot have comforted the countless small children drowned in springs, water-holes and special parts of Lake Texcoco to rejuvenate the water-gods.

Some humans became very strongly associated with animal spirits, while retaining human shape. The Mother of Game of the eastern Pueblos led the deer, mountain goats, buffalo and hares in an annual dance promising successful hunting. And Sedna of the eastern Eskimos was an undersea woman who owned the sea-mammals on which the Eskimos lived. Originally she was a human girl who married a dog and then a petrel. These eccentric tastes were disapproved of by her father, who stole her from the petrel and escaped in a canoe. The petrel raised a violent storm, and to save himself the father immediately threw his daughter overboard. As Sedna clung desperately to the side of the canoe, her loving father chopped off her finger-joints one by one – and these became the seals and walruses which ever afterwards lived under the care of the Old Mother, as she became known.

Animals and their Elder Brothers are on the whole friendly to man, provided he observes the proper ceremonies of homage. But the Cherokee Indians in South Carolina have a myth which betrays a certain impatience. As man began to trap more and more animals, threatening to extinguish them altogether, they all met to discuss what was to be done. Each species invented a different disease with which to attack man in his turn. The hunters would have been decimated by attacks of measles and influenza had not the plants, which were also present, taken pity on them, each agreeing to provide a remedy for one of the animals' diseases.

All descriptions of the afterworlds of the Indians are a little vague. The Happy Hunting Ground was never celebrated by anyone other than hunters, and some of them had never heard of it. Some tribes of American Indians thought of the afterworld as a shadowy village where homesick dead lived, longing to be joined by their loved ones. The Alaskan

Xochipilli, who despite having the head of a corpse, is Prince of Flowers, god of happiness, love, youth, dancing and gambling

Eskimos played football in the glow of the Aurora Borealis; the Navaho dead seem simply to have become part of organic life, their dust poured into the desert dust. It was generally assumed that there would be some sort of afterlife, however, bringing man into contact with the spirit-gods as he became, like them, immortal. Sometimes, like the Egyptians, the Indians made elaborate preparations for their illustrious dead against the fateful meeting. The Muisca, a tribe which inhabited the Bogata plateau of Colombia (and a group of people with somewhat unpleasant habits, such as that of driving the

supporting piers of their palaces into the ground through the living bodies of young girls), took great care with the bodies of their aristocrats, mummifying and burying them with their wives and attendants ranged in layers above them. Sometimes the bodies of Muisca kings were carried into battle at the head of their warriors, inspiring them with courage.

Most Indians believed that a man had two souls – the one which died when the body died, and the one which was free to wander about in dreams, or to leave a person when he was ill and which would then have to be sought by a doctor and recovered, to ensure a return to health. There were tribes who believed there was a soul in every joint of the body, for did not every joint separately feel pain?

The thunderbird played a prominent part in most Indian mythologies. Almost always birds were associated with thunder, and the thunderbirds lived in the upper regions of clouds and winds – invisible spirits occasionally signalling their presence, flashing their eyes in lightning or beating their wings in thunder. A few minor thunderbirds actually came low enough to be seen, golden eagles among them. And mountain Indians identified small red birds shooting lightning from their wings.

The Pacific Indians believed in a most superior thunderbird, vast enough to carry a whole lake on its back, from which the waters occasionally spilled in rain. This super-thunderbird ate whales, leaving the bones on the tops of mountains to perplex anthropologists. It was no relation, however, to the huge bird Nunyunc, which carried off men; nor to the Piasa, a man-eating bird whose image is carved in the rocks at Alton, Illinois. Nor was there a connection with the appealing thunder-god Haokah, of the Dakota Sioux, a drummer who used the winds as sticks to beat his thunder-drum. He would bow his horned head and weep when he was happy, and would laugh when he was sad. Heat made him shiver, and cold made him sweat.

The strong narrative lines of the legends of, say, the Iroquois do not exist in every Indian tribe. The Sun, presiding over a large pantheon of immortals, acts as a unifying force; but his pantheon is a confused, Babel-ish one. Among the Zuni of New Mexico he ruled the Uwanami, or rainmakers, who lived on the very edge of the world; the Wemawe, or animal-gods; the Koko, or mask-gods; and the Ahayuta, or war-gods. And the various Zuni tribes

(the Taos, San Juan, Santa Clara, San Idlefonso and others) all had their own legends.

The gods of the Pueblos are less personal than those of other North American tribes; but there are exceptions. The Kwakiutl have very real and individual gods, such as the formidable Baxbakwalanuxsiwae ('The Cannibal at the North End of the World'), who feeds on human beings and lives in the exact north of the world, where red smoke can be seen rising from the roof of his house. When the autumn storms get up, he comes southward to visit mortals, before whom he appears to dance forbiddingly, masked and emitting his cry of *Hap! Hap!* (Eat! Eat!).

Some Mexican gods were extremely vicious: the dreadful Tlalocan, god of mountain and rain, had to be placated by the sacrifice of as many human babies as possible. If they were not yet weaned, so much the better; and the more noise they made as they were being sacrificed, the better the chance of rain.

The Mayas of Yucatan worshipped a sun-god, Hunab Ku, whose son Itzamna, a literate and cultured immortal, had the power of granting immortality. And they had many other gods: the Becabs, or piers of heaven; Chin, the god of lust; and Nohochacyumchac, god of all creation. The Guatemalans worshipped sun- and moon-gods, and also the fire-god Hurakan, whose cult spread to the West Indies and who made fire by rubbing his sandals together.

The all-embracing power of the sun, personified as a god in so many great religions, was seen in central Colombia in the god Bochica, who defeated the wicked devil Chibchacum in single combat, and forced him to carry the world on his shoulder (when he shifts the weight to the other shoulder, there is an earthquake).

Worship in the empire of the Incas again centred on the Sun, Inti or Apu-Punchau, with his dazzlingly beautiful human body, and his head circled by a great blaze of gold. The Incas were descended from him in direct line, and only they were allowed to pronounce his name. Inti plunged into the sea every evening, to vanish for the night, which he spent swimming under the earth, to emerge in the early morning refreshed by his cold dip.

Eupai, god of the dark underworld, was greedy for subjects, and by inventing death persuaded the

A Kachina, from the Hopi Indians of Arizona. Kachinas bear prayers from man to the gods

Overleaf: The classical Roman Jupiter, from a statue in the Vatican Museum

vast majority of human beings eventually to join him. A hundred children a year were sacrificed to placate him. Growing up in the Inca civilization must have been an exceptionally chancy business.

The mythical beasts (as opposed to the spirit-animals) of the American Indian mythology compete with the unicorn and basilisk of Europe for strangeness. The Pueblos lived in fear of the Achiyalabopa, with his feathers like knives, or of the Ahuizotle, a Thing which would range the river-banks of Mexico. About the size of a large dog, it would cry like a human child; but when anyone approached to investigate, it would seize them by a monkey's hand on the end of its large flexible tail and make off with them. After three days, a corpse would be found minus eyes, teeth and nails – tidbits to the Ahuizotle.

The Anaye were the bane of the Navaho Indians. A selection of giants and monsters born of virgins, they included: the Great Hairy Thelgeth (who had no head), the Feathered Harpy of Tsanahale; the legless and armless twins, the Binaye Ahani, who fortunately for them were able to slay with a basilisk glare of their eyes; and there was an extremely unfelicitous monster whose hair grew into the sides of a cliff (thus preventing it from falling off), and who preyed on travellers.

The Cocoa, one of the very few cat immortals of America, haunted the Quechua Indians of Peru. Only two feet long, with a tail half that length again and marked with stripes, it had a large head from whose doleful eyes continual hail rained to the ground.

Chac was an Indian rain-god, with two intertwined serpents instead of a head. He lived on top of a mountain, where he ran a home for warriors killed in battle and women dead in childbed. He took particular care of the drowned, and, as rain-god, was much concerned with fertility.

The Nicmac Indians of eastern Canada often came across the Halfway People. Closely related to mermaids, they had human (not exclusively female) upper parts and fishes' tails, and sang before storms as a warning. If sufficiently irritated, they themselves could raise storms.

An unpleasant sea-beast was the southern American Cuero, a giant octopus with claws at the end of its tentacles, its ears covered with eyes which could become large or small at will.

117

GODLY COMPARISONS

If one takes the Greek pantheon to stand at the centre of world mythology – where it surely belongs because of its complex structure and enormous influence – it is possible to follow certain themes in the characters and personalities of the Greek gods and goddesses through the mythologies of other civilizations, and to discover what looks very like a world-wide immortal hierarchy. Zeus, for instance, became Jupiter to the Romans, and we can find him thinly disguised as the Hindu Dyaus, the Egyptian Amon, the Assyro-Babylonian Enlil, the Teutonic Tyr, the Chinese August Personage of Jade and, surprisingly, the female Japanese sun-goddess Amaterasu.

None of these were 'creator-gods': they all had predecessors connected with creation myths. They represented rather a stabilizing of myth: by the time they had evolved, and their fellow-gods lower down the scale, humankind had had time to rationalize its feelings about the way the world might have begun, how the universe might operate. Human beings too by then wanted a set of gods they could invest with human characteristics to justify their own weaknesses and failings, their own rashness, irritability or heroism. How often do the gods go out on the rampage, seducing beautiful maidens, stealing and lying and arguing. If they can do it, why can't man? The dogmas of kindness, charity, human dignity – the rationale of Jesus rather than of Jehovah, who bears a strong resemblance to Zeus and his contemporaries – are still centuries away. Mankind is not yet ready for them.

The Zeus syndrome

The Romans, great copiers, who usually managed to overlay the delicacy and refinement of what they copied with their own rather stolid style, simply renamed Zeus Jupiter, not even altering the myth of his origin very much. Rhea was still his mother, though his father, Cronus to the Greeks, became Saturn.

The Hindu Dyaus was preceded by 'creation'-figures, but himself became very much the same kind of father-figure as Zeus. Amon, the Egyptian, was again not an originator or maker of the world, but took a Zeusian place, with Ra, as a definite king of gods. The Assyro-Babylonian Zeus-figure is Enlil (or, ruling over the land of Sumer, Bel), while the strictly Babylonian Lord of the World was the great Marduk, who sent earthly kings to rule as his ambassadors, underlining the fact that most of the father-figure gods were strongly connected with events on earth, and with earthly emotions.

Tyr, the Teutonic Zeus, born from the sweat of Ymir, father of the giants, was of the same hierarchy as Donar and Woden; he was associated with the light of heaven itself. He had some association with the ideal of legal government (as did Jupiter), but later was more concerned with battle, filling an ideal which might more strictly have been that of Mars.

In the Far East, the Zeus concept expresses itself in the beautiful Chinese myth of the August Personage of Jade, who reigns second in a supreme triad, preceded by the Heavenly Master of the First Origin, and followed by the Dawn of Jade of the Golden Door. The Japanese sun-goddess Amaterasu occupied first place in official Japanese mythology, though she was not entirely omnipotent and seems to have been rather more ladylike than her colleagues. Her ancestry is easily traced to the fundamental Japanese creation myths, while her line can be traced forward to the birth of the present emperor.

The Mars syndrome

The concept of the war-god is omnipresent in the various pantheons of mythology, signifying man's apparently constant preoccupation with war. Ares, the Greek, was totally a god of war and battle – indeed so purely interested in strife that he was the most unpopular and unlikeable of the Olympians. (Incidentally, he seems to have grown younger as the years went by: the earliest portraits show him as an armour-clad bearded veteran; but later ones portray him as a beardless youth.)

Ares became Mars in Roman mythology, and assumed much greater importance with the many battles fought to establish the empire. A large number of Roman victories bolstered his reputation, and he eclipsed even Jupiter in popularity and importance.

In Indian mythology Indra seems most to resemble Mars. He was a warrior-god, but also god of the weather; he rode through the skies singing war songs, and was adept at slaying dragons. Pyerun, in Slavonic myth, was also associated with the skies – with thunder, the Polish word for which is *piorun*, the thunderbolt often being considered a divine weapon. In Teutonic mythology Donar was the god of thunder, but Wotan was more in command of the pantheon. He had strong military

121

preoccupations, but was also extremely wise, and in the northern countries (where his name was Odin) was the god of intelligence, in charge of the laws of humanity – like Jupiter and Tyr. Like Jupiter, too, he was in the habit of transforming himself into many guises. But it is a Martian character he finally assumes.

Another god strongly resembling Mars is the Egyptian Anhur, something of a warlike Ra, but with the warrior characteristics of Ares – though he was regarded as the Good Warrior, and obviously had a more pleasant persona than his Greek original. He spent a great deal of time hunting down dangerous animals.

Mars the god became Mars the planet, and it is not surprising that when he appears in Persian mythology it is in a direct astrological connotation: astrological Martian qualities provide a pen-picture of the behaviour of Ares and his fellows.

The Venus syndrome

The concept of the Love Goddess is one which has survived time: in the coronations of beauty queens, in the adulation of Greta Garbo, Marilyn Monroe and other film beauties, we see the same impulse that went to the creation of Aphrodite, the child of Zeus and Dione (according to Homer), or a woman who rose pure and beautiful from the bloody spume of the sea, the direct result of the castration of a male (according to another, perhaps significant, myth).

The goddess of love and beauty and the divine patron of marriage, Aphrodite was much connected also with fertility cults. In the Roman pantheon she became Venus, and the discovery of the Venus de Milo in 1820 has placed her firmly in the twentieth-century mind as the epitome of womanly beauty. In the mythology of the Phoenicians she appeared as Ashtart, and in Mesopotamia as Ishtar. Mesopotamian carvings often show her with a crescent moon on her head, and that symbol is often connected with her: it is, of course, the symbol of motherhood – in astrology the planet Venus rules the two signs of the zodiac most connected with love, with personal relationships, and with beauty (Taurus and Libra) – and is 'exalted' in Taurus.

In Indian mythology she crops up as the goddess Lakshmi or Sri, who is perhaps rather more worldly than Aphrodite, for besides being the goddess of feminine beauty, she also looks after 'fortune' and prosperity.

The Mercury syndrome

Hermes, the Greek original of Mercury, was of
extremely ancient Thracian origin, particularly
revered by Arcadian shepherds. But he was best
known as the messenger of the gods, with a special
responsibility for travellers and journeys. His
connection with trade is stressed, too (perhaps
because most journeys, in the earliest times, were
taken for reasons of business – or, of course, war or
love). He was also the god of eloquence (again, the
connection with trade may provide an explanation
for this). In the Roman pantheon he became
Mercury, and perhaps is better known under that
name (just as Aphrodite is better known as Venus).
The name derives from the Latin for 'goods' and
'payment'. As was the case with Mars, he tends to
grow younger as one looks at carvings of him: first

he is bearded and rather sedate, later beardless, a
young athlete.

Though Wagner, in his *Ring,* made Loge a quick-
talking deceitful go-between (Mercurial traits),
there is little to justify the Teutonic Loki in the role
of messenger. The Egyptian Thoth was certainly
one – a spokesman, too, and a keeper of records, the
patron of science, literature, wisdom and inventions.
The vizier of Osiris and later Horus, he was
Mercurial enough; and when Horus retired, Thoth
succeeded to the throne and reigned peacefully for
no less than 3,226 years.

The concept of a god-messenger is not a very
widespread one: the Japanese have their gods of the
road, including Chimata-No-Kami, protector of
crossroads; but not in the same order as Hermes.

The SAINTS

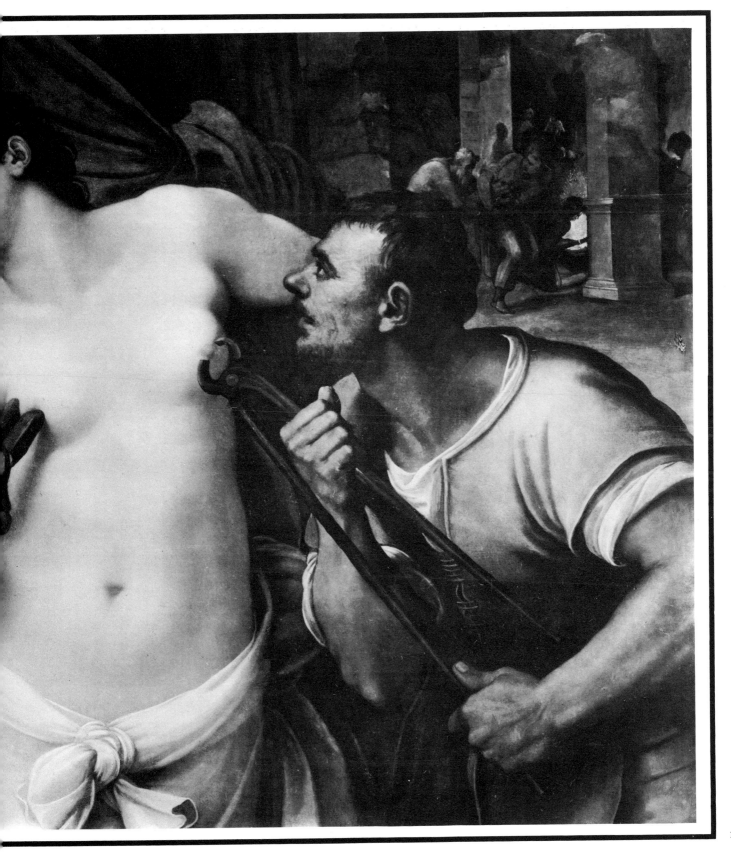

Christianity asserts that we are all immortal. Nevertheless, a number of Christian saints qualify for inclusion in any list of mythical immortals, for the Catholic Church freely admits that they never existed as individuals.

Since modern historical methods were applied to the study of the general Calendar of the Church, it has been realized that the legendary lives of saints were more common than had been supposed. Ancient writers composed biographies of often non-existent Christian heroes simply for the edification and pleasure of their readers. (They also invented various miracles supposed to have been performed by saints who undoubtedly did exist.) There was a considerable sense of shock when, comparatively recently, the Vatican removed St George from the Calendar at least partly because there is no evidence to show that he existed.

The lives of imaginary saints, however, are worth reading – not necessarily for instruction, but certainly for pleasure, just as one reads the stories of the Greek gods. *The Golden Legend*, a book of saints' lives written in the thirteenth century by James of Voragine, remained a best-seller for some years after its first printing in 1470, and of it Father Hippolyte Delehaye, a distinguished hagiographer, was to write five hundred years later: 'I confess that, when reading it, it is often difficult to refrain from smiling. But it is a sympathetic and friendly smile, which does not at all disturb the religious response aroused by the picture of the goodness and heroic deeds of the saints.'

St Afra   The Emperor Diocletian, rounding up prostitutes in about AD 300, arrested among others the young Afra. When she was ordered to be sacrificed to the gods, she replied coolly: 'My body has sinned, let it suffer – I will not corrupt my soul by idolatry.' She was burned to death, or so the legend goes, for there is no evidence that she ever existed.

St Agatha   While there was certainly a martyr called Agatha in Sicily, there is no proof that her legend is true. In it, she is said to have been a beautiful and noble young woman wooed by a consul, Quintian. She rejected him, and he prosecuted her for Christianity. While she was being tortured, St Peter appeared in a vision to comfort her; but she died, nevertheless. Among other tortures, her breasts are said to have been cut off,

Left: St Euphrosyne, unusually shown wearing woman's clothes from an early manuscript

Right: St Paphnutius calling at the home of the reformed harlot, St Thais. From a painting by Philippe de Champaigne (1602–74)

Bottom: St Cecilia lies, only a thin line showing where her neck was severed, in a catacomb beneath the Roman Appian Way

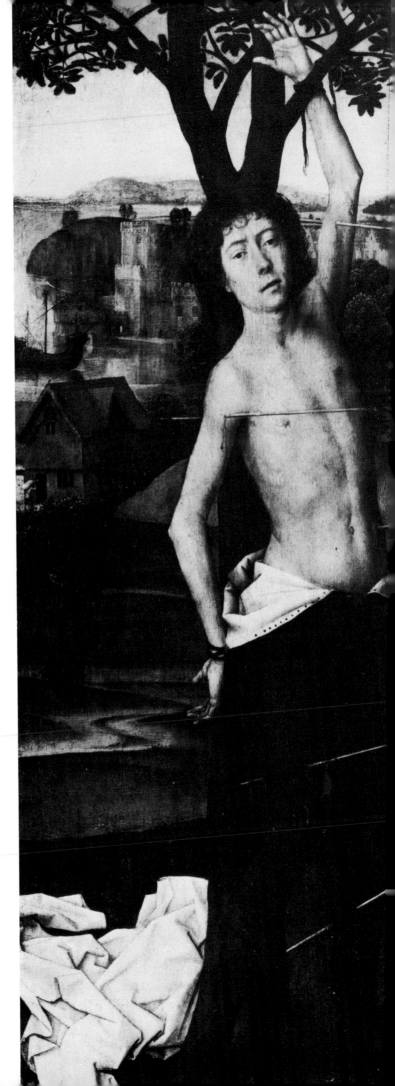

Sublimely ignoring the arrows puncturing his flesh.
St Sebastian undergoes martyrdom. Painting by
Hans Memling (1430–1494)

and in some early pictures she is shown carrying
them on a tray. One indifferent painter made them
look rather like bells, and she was promptly adopted
as the patron saint of bell-founders! Another bad
painting made her breasts look like loaves of bread,
and this led to the custom of blessing bread on her
feast-day, which is 5 February.

St Amadour Supposed to have been a servant of
the Virgin Mary, Amadour apparently married St
Veronica (also a mythical saint), and founded a
shrine at Rocamadour in France.

St Attracta A number of surprising miracles were
attributed to this imaginary Irish saint, who
founded a shelter for travellers at Killaraght. Her
activities spread over two centuries.

St Barbara The *Golden Legend* tells the story of
a young girl of legendary beauty whose father,
Dioscurus, imprisoned her in a high tower to
discourage her many suitors. Discovering that she
had by some means been converted to Christianity,
he determined to kill her, but she miraculously
floated from the tower to safety. Caught by the
authorities, she was tortured, refused to recant, and
her father was told to execute her. He struck off her
head, and was himself instantly struck by lightning
and reduced to ashes. St Barbara was adopted as a
saint particularly good at protecting the faithful
from lightning, and as patron saint of gunners.

SS Barlaam and Josaphat Josaphat is said to have
been the son of an Indian monarch, who closely shut
him up against the possibility of his being
converted. Barlaam managed to reach him, and
indeed converted him. When he succeeded his
father, Josaphat declined to take the throne, and he
and Barlaam lived happily ever afterwards as
hermits. The story seems to have originally
appeared in Arabic, and is very like that of
Siddhartha Buddha. It may have originated in
India.

St Benignus Some bones found in an ancient tomb
at Dijon were said to have been that of Benignus, a
second-century martyr. It is just possible that the
original Benignus may have been a missionary from
Lyons; but the stories told about him are all
legendary.

St Cassian of Imola Cassian is said to have been a Christian schoolmaster who, on declining to make sacrifice to the gods, was handed over to his pupils, who promptly stabbed him to death with their pens.

St Cecilia A moving statue of the alleged St Cecilia, patron saint of music, is to be seen in the catacombs in Rome. She was said to have been an upper-class Christian girl who on her wedding day converted her bridegroom, Valerian. Valerian's brother Tiburtius was also converted, and the brothers were baptized together. Shortly afterwards they were arrested and put to death. Cecilia too was brought before the priests, and sentenced to be stifled in her own bathroom. The water-heating system declined to operate at sufficient pressure, however, and she was beheaded instead. Later the bathroom became a chapel. There were certainly two martyrs called Valerian and Tiburtius, but there is no record of any Cecilia reliable enough to be trusted. Nor is there any reason why she became the patroness of music, except that the earliest version of her story speaks of her singing in her heart as the music played at her wedding.

SS Chrysanthus and Daria Chrysanthus was a handsome young Roman boy whose father persuaded a priestess of Minerva, the beautiful and sensual Daria, to attempt to seduce him from Christianity. Instead, in one way or another, he converted her, and they were married. Remaining virgins, they set an example so moving and pure that a whole troop of soldiers was converted by them. Consequently they were all beheaded, and Chrysanthus and Daria themselves were buried alive in a sand-pit. A number of Christians came to pray over their bodies, and were walled up alive.

SS Cosmas and Damian There is some reason to suppose that the story of these two saints is really a version of the story of the Dioscuri, the twin sons of Zeus. They were two brothers who practised medicine without charging for their services. This, no less than the fact that they were obstinate Christians, upset the general medical council of the time, and they were martyred. One of their habits was to send sick people to sleep in a Christian church, on the understanding that they would dream of the proper method of curing themselves.

St Cuthman When his father died, the young English shepherd Cuthman decided to travel from the westcountry to Steyning, in Sussex. His aged mother was still alive and he took her along in a handcart. At Steyning he built a small church. Christopher Fry's play *The Boy with a Cart* serves as a biography of him.

St Dorothy Two women sent to Dorothy to convert her from Christianity on the orders of Diocletian, were converted themselves. As she was being led to her own execution she met a jeering lawyer, Theophilus, who asked her to send him some fruit and flowers from heaven when she got there. A child immediately appeared with some roses and apples, and Theophilus was converted on the spot. He was martyred not long after Dorothy.

St Dympna When the wife of a certain Irish king died, he fell passionately in love with his daughter, Dympna, who took ship immediately for Belgium with her chaplain, Gerebernus. Her father pursued her, and when she failed to respond to his wooing, killed both her and the priest. She became, for no

St Ursula, in a late fifteenth-century painting, supports a woebegun dead friend while, behind her, the Huns mercilessly martyr her 11,000 virgins. She remains indifferent to the approaches of the Hun commander, by submitting to whose blandishments she could save her friends

very good reason, patroness of the insane, and one admirable result of her cult is that a mental hospital was founded in her honour at Gheel, near Antwerp, where since medieval times it has sustained a reputation for being among the best places in the world for the examination and treatment of mental disorders.

St Erasmus of Elmo   An original martyrdom was invented for this imaginary saint. He died, it is said, after having his intestines wound out of his body on a windlass, and for that reason he became the patron saint of sailors. When 'St Elmo's fire' was seen dancing at the mast-heads of ships – an electrical phenomenon fairly common at sea – it was taken as a sign of his special protection.

St Eulalia   The best-known (if fictional) martyred saint of Spain, St Eulalia was believed to have been a twelve-year-old child who spoke up against the magistrates busily condemning Christians during Maximilian's persecution in the fourth century. She

was tortured and burned to death. However, at the moment of her death, a white dove flew from her mouth; and when her body was taken from the stake, snow fell to cover the blackened remains.

St Euphrosyne   Threatened with marriage, Euphrosyne dressed herself as a man and joined a monastery near Alexandria, calling herself Brother Smaragdus. Her father confessed to her and took her as his adviser for many years without recognizing her. When she was dying she revealed her identity, and he took over her cell.

St Eustace   Out hunting near Tivoli, one of Trajan's generals saw a luminous crucifix growing from the head of a stag. Converted, he spent some years deprived of command, and penniless. Restored to his position, he led his converted troops to victory, but on declining to make sacrifice to the gods in thanksgiving, he and his family were roasted to death.

St Expeditus   One story goes that a box of relics sent from Rome to Paris in the nineteenth century bore the word *spedito* (or 'sent off'), and that this was mistaken by the receiving monks for the name of the saint whose bones were enclosed. But this is only a guess at the origin of a wholly fictional saint.

St Febriona   When the Prefect Selenus was rampaging through Mesopotamia carrying out the Emperor Diocletian's orders to stamp out Christianity, he was particularly impressed by the beauty and courage of one Christian girl, Febriona, who lived at Nisibis. Selenus had a nephew of some talent, but inclined towards Christianity. To teach them both a lesson, Selenus offered her freedom if she married Lysimachus (she would undoubtedly recant to save her skin, and Lysimachus would see what her Christianity was worth). To his surprise, she refused, preferring to be tortured, mutilated and battered to death. Lysimachus was converted, together with a large number of others, and baptized.

SS Florus and Laurus   This euphonious pair are said to be distantly related to the pagan Castor and Pollux, though their respective legends bear no resemblance to each other. They were allegedly twin Greek brothers working as builders on a heathen temple. Converted to Christianity during these operations, they had no sooner completed the

131

temple than they began tearing it down. The Emperor Licinius thereupon ordered that they and their unfortunate employers, Proculus and Maximus, should be put down a well.

St Genesius the Actor   During an engagement in Rome, Genesius, an actor, played the part in a satire of a Christian being baptized. Introduced afterwards to the Emperor Diocletian, he mentioned in conversation that he had been converted during the performance. Diocletian was the wrong emperor to have received this confidence, and Genesius lost the part and his head. Unsurprisingly, a number of dramatists, including Lope de Vega, have written plays about him.

St George   The *Golden Legend* is one of the chief sources of the St George legend, telling the story of the brave and handsome Cappadocian knight who at Silene in Libya slew a fiery dragon and rescued a beautiful maiden. Diocletian (responsible, it seems, almost single-handedly for the deaths of most fictional martyrs) put him to death at Nicomedia. His name was known in England from a very early date, and knights returning from the Crusades made his legend popular. King Edward III made him

patron of the Order of the Garter, and it may have been at that time, in the fourteenth century, that he became known as patron saint of England. His feast-day, 23 April, was of paramount importance for five hundred years, until in 1960 he was demoted by the Vatican and an order issued that his name should simply be mentioned, in passing as it were, at mass and lauds.

SS Joachim and Ann   Allegedly the parents of the Virgin Mary, taken from a very early manuscript, the *Protevangelium of James*. There is no reason to believe that, as those two people at all events, they ever existed.

St Catherine of Alexandria   A noble, wise, and very beautiful virgin (an ignorant and ugly saint is extraordinarily difficult to find), Catherine lived in Alexandria, and protested to the Emperor, Maxentius, about the public worship of idols. Fifty leading philosophers of the country argued with her, and on being publicly and ignominiously defeated were burnt alive for their failure to confute her. The Emperor then proposed to her, and when she rejected him, he had her beaten for two hours and imprisoned. Starved, she was brought food by a dove. She was bound to a wheel (hence catherine-wheel), but it fell to pieces, injuring several spectators. Two hundred soldiers, looking on, were instantly converted and speedily beheaded, as was she.

St Margaret   The Prefect Olybrius fell in love with Margaret, the daughter of a pagan priest at Antioch. Rejected, he denounced her as a Christian, and she was taken to be tortured. In the middle of her sufferings, the Devil appeared, disguised as a dragon, and swallowed her. She reappeared, however, and was beheaded by Diocletian's soldiers.

St Marina   When Marina's father became a monk, in Bithynia, she stayed with him disguised as a boy. When he died, she remained in the monastery and was accused of seducing a local innkeeper's daughter, who became pregnant. She did penance for five years, and her innocence was only discovered after her death. (Donald Attwater in his *Dictionary of Saints* points out that there was a girl, Hildegund, who lived in a German monastery in disguise until her death in 1188; but she has no connection with the fictional St Marina.)

St Mark of Arethusa   Another schoolmaster stabbed to death by his pupils' pens (*see* St Cassian of Imola).

St Nicephorus of Antioch   Nicephorus had a quarrel with an Antioch priest, Sapricius. He apologized several times, but Sapricius declined to shake hands. Arrested and accused of Christianity, the priest met Nicephorus on the way to his execution, and the layman again attempted to apologize. On the scaffold, Sapricius suddenly decided to recant, and offered to make a sacrifice to the gods if his life was spared. Nicephorus, in the audience, was outraged, shouted at him to take his medicine, and eventually maintained (quite falsely, as far as one can tell) that he was a Christian, and was executed in Sapricius' place. An example, on the face of it, of quite unexampled blockheaded stubbornness.

St Nino the Slave-girl   When Nino, a slave-girl, was captured and taken to Iberia in the fourth century, the Iberians were impressed by the number of cures she was able to effect in the name of her god, Jesus. The Queen herself had been cured by Nino, and the King, lost while hunting, thought it worthwhile calling on Christ for directions. He

found his way home safely, took tuition from the girl, became a Christian and built a church. During the building, the masons received such an amount of supernatural help that they and a great number of Iberians were converted.

St Pelagia the Penitent   Bishop Nonnus of Edessa was one day watching the unspeakably licentious dancing of Pelagia, in a place of low repute in Antioch. 'This girl is a lesson to us bishops,' he concluded. 'She takes more trouble over her body than we do over our souls and our flock.' Pelagia happened to be in church shortly afterwards, was converted by the Bishop, promptly dressed herself as a man and went to live in a cave on the Mount of Olives.

Palagia of Tarsus   The son of the most famous persecutor of Christians, the Emperor Diocletian, is said to have had a son who fell in love with a beautiful girl called Pelagia. Just after the engagement was announced, she became a Christian, and her fiancé killed himself for shame. Diocletian, true to his reputation, attempted to seduce her, and when she refused him, roasted her inside a brazen bull.

SS Rhipsime and Gaiana   The Emperor Diocletian cast his eyes upon a beautiful girl, Rhipsime, who happened to be a Christian. Her friend Gaiana got together a small band of Christian women, and fled with Rhipsime to Armenia, where King Tiridates also fancied Rhipsime. When she rejected him, he slaughtered the entire company.

St Sebastian   With St George, perhaps the most famous apocryphal saint. Born in Gaul, he allegedly became an officer in the Royal Imperial Guard. When the Emperor Diocletian, that ubiquitous Christian-hater, discovered his true religion, he sentenced him to be shot to death with arrows. Left for dead with innumerable arrow-wounds, he was picked up by the widow of another martyr, St Castulus, only to be battered to death by clubs when Diocletian discovered his escape. His martyrdom has attracted the attention of innumerable artists, which has helped to make his legend famous.

The Seven Sleepers   In the third century, seven Christians were said to have been walled up alive. There they fell asleep, awakening two centuries later. The story is related in *The Golden Legend*.

133

Right: Ss Rhipsime and Gaiana executed by a servant of King Tiridates
Below: General, later St Eustace, out at chase with his dogs, discovers the stag with the luminous crucifix. Painting by Antonio Pisanello (*c* 1395–1455).

St Susan A niece of St Caius, Bishop of Rome, Susan was beheaded when she turned down the hand (or perhaps just the approaches) of Maximilian, a friend of the Emperor Diocletian. Her father and two uncles joined her in martyrdom.

St Thais An extremely well-known and often-visited whore, Thais became extremely wealthy. In Egypt, where she was a prominent citizen, there also lived a desert monk (perhaps St Paphnutius), who decided he ought to try to convert her. For a reason which remains unclear, he was successful at his first attempt. Thais burned all her jewels and fine clothes and was escorted to a nunnery, where she lived happily for three years before an exemplary death.

St Ursula Ursula, daughter of an English king, swept out of the country with her retinue when he tried to force her into an unwanted marriage. The party stayed for a while in Rome, but on their way home all were killed by a band of marauding Huns, because they had become Christians. The earliest versions of the story say that Ursula had ten companions; later, she was said to have had eleven thousand virgins with her – which in the state of Europe at the time seems, for all sorts of reasons, improbable.

St Veronica One of the original myths of Christ's passion, that which tells how Veronica, a woman of Jerusalem, took pity on Christ as he carried his cross through the streets and wiped his face with a cloth, on which his features became indelibly printed, seems on the strength of the evidence (or lack of it) to be a legend. Although for many centuries St Veronica's original cloth has been preserved in St Peter's, Rome, her name does not appear in the Martyrology, and it seems she never existed.

St Vitus Diocletian was responsible for Vitus' death. An inhabitant of Sicily, he perished with his Christian nurse Crescentia and her husband Modestus. His name guards against epilepsy and St Vitus's dance (*chorea*).

St Wilgefortis The King of Portugal betrothed his daughter Wilgefortis to the King of Sicily. She had determined to remain a virgin, and in answer to her impassioned prayers a beard grew on her face, which, not surprisingly, put the King of Sicily off. Her father promptly crucified her.

The DEVIL

The Fall of the Rebel Angels by Pieter Bruegel (*c* 1525–69)

In the most primitive religions there are evil
spirits, and as the hierarchy of those spirits in the
religions of early man became clearer and more
defined, so leaders of the evil forces began to
emerge. For our own epoch it is Christianity which
has presented the arch-demon of all, Satan himself:
the Devil.

At first, he was a rather shadowy figure. In the
Book of Job (written perhaps in about 450 BC) he is
still on social terms with God: 'Now there was a day
when the sons of God came to present themselves
before the Lord, and Satan also came among them.'
He spent his time 'going to and fro in the earth, and
walking up and down in it'. (And indeed sometimes
still he leaves visible signs of his wanderings, as
when in 1855, during a cold English winter, the
footprints of an unknown Thing were traced for
over a hundred miles through the snow from Totnes
to Littlehampton, in the English westcountry.) But
the ancient Jehovah still retained a dual nature – he
was good and evil ('I form the light, and create
darkness: I make peace, and create evil'). As God
himself became milder and kindlier, the Devil
became evil incarnate, and the emergence of Jesus
threw him into even stronger relief.

The early Christians saw him everywhere: he was
the dark force behind the worship of Jove and
Minerva, Venus and Mars; his voice was heard in
the roaring of the lions in the Colosseum; the clatter
of his armour and the flash of his sword announced
the searchers in the catacombs. He prospered
particularly in times of uncertainty, and reigned
almost supreme in the Middle Ages, when man, his
life overshadowed by disease and famine and death,
witnessed his presence in many different places.
Religious leaders saw him lurking in the shadows of
cathedrals, and knew that he could inhabit the north
side of churches, where often a little door was
considerately left open so that he could flee during
Communion. The hermit or saint saw him in
visions; the poor themselves seemed already to be in
his clutches, he was so fearfully omnipresent to
them. The demons of Greece and Rome seemed by
comparison to have operated in bright sunlight –
there was a mischievousness, a cheerfulness in their
escapades. The Devil of Christian myth was
ultimately unpleasant.

His antecedents are a little vague – in the Old
Testament he is seen as a disturber and corrupter of
the work of God, who through envy persuaded
Adam and Eve to sin. Michael, the Archangel, took

Left: Kali, wife of Siva, goddess of death: black, four-armed, with red palms and eyes and bloodstained matted hair and a necklace of corpses' heads

Below: Satan and the waters of the burning lake. A vision by 'Mad' John Martin (1789–1854), illustrating Milton

him on, and he fell as lightning from heaven. But though defeated, he can still prowl and prowl around, and St Paul tells us that evil men will even be handed over to him for punishment – though hell itself is undoubtedly reserved for ultimate damnation.

It is in the New Testament that his personality becomes clearer. There he is a person rather than an abstraction, manifesting himself to tempt Jesus, persuading Judas to betrayal, with his own synagogue (as reported in Revelations), a master of disguise (able, for instance, to impersonate an angel of light), and with his own band of 'angels' or ministers, and able to make his own converts. He should not, then, be underestimated. He is extremely clever, and extremely powerful – he can read one's thoughts and prey upon them; he is omnipresent, taking advantage of every momentary weakness; he is 'the god of this world' in command of all evil things, 'principalities, powers, rulers of the darkness of this world, and spiritual powers in heavenly places'.

The Devil is the ugliest of immortals, his basically human shape disfigured and horrid. The imaginations of poets and painters have endowed him with almost every graceless appendage: the horns of an ox, the ears of an ass, a tail ending in serpent's jaws, a body covered with ugly, grinning miniature faces, goat's legs, feet like vultures' talons, and a coiled, twisted and razor-sharp phallus. He was once believed to be hollow, like a tree-trunk rotted away, and early saints who actually met him have added more details. St Fursey (an Irishman who founded monasteries in England and France, and was given – the Venerable Bede says – to falling into trances) described his head as being like a brazen cauldron; St Guthlac (an English teetotaller) spoke of flames spouting from his every bodily orifice; and St Brigitta of feet like grappling-irons.

There are a few exceptions: artists and writers who saw in the Devil more than a trace of the angel he was before his fall, when he was still beloved of God. This is how the fourteenth-century Bishop Federigo Frezzi saw him, in his poem *Quadriregio*:

> *Stately he was, and fair, and so benign*
> *His aspect, and with majesty so filled*
> *That of all reverence he appeared most worthy.*

But one cannot help feeling that he was imposing on the good Bishop: there is ample evidence that he can 141 adopt a shining aspect if it suits him. One member of a famous religious French family, Mary de Maillé, recognized him disguised as a venerable and much-admired holy man, who was instantly condemned; the blessed Gherardesca of Pisa saw through him when he appeared to her disguised as her husband (history does not recount what happened to him); and when an extremely handsome and well-endowed young man was seen sneaking nakedly from the bedroom of St Kunegund, it was of course instantly recognized that he was the Devil in disguise (or that was the opinion of her husband, Henry II, a Holy Roman Emperor). Similarly, when St Silvanus, Bishop of Nazareth, was discovered under a young girl's bed in the small hours, it was obvious who really hid within his skin.

Like Jupiter, a much more amiable adulterer, the Devil is very good at animal impersonations: he has been recognized disguised as a dragon, a fly, a fox, an ant and many other creatures. St Giles, a French hermit whose life-story contains wonderful anachronisms, once saw him dressed as an enormous tortoise; and as a dog, he became for a while a friend and mentor of Pope Silvanus II. Fortunately, holy men have generally recognized him before much damage has been done, and St Patrick, St Geoffrey, St Bernard and a number of other saints are on record as excommunicating flies, reptiles and animals which, they realized, was their enemy in disguise. The most recent example recorded seems to have been in 1474, when the worthy magistrates of Basle burned alive a cock unwise enough, or perhaps talented enough, to lay an egg, and thus betray his diabolic personality.

The Devil's main occupation, of course, is to tempt. He is a past master at offering acceptable bribes – beautiful flesh to the lustful, gold and silver (or, one supposes, uranium or oil) to the avaricious . . . it is a talent he has always had. St Pelagia the Penitent, once a notoriously licentious dancing-girl and 'actress', was tempted with the paste jewellery and baubles of her former art. While St Hilarion, who had set himself up as a hermit in a hut in Gaza and fasted, had a rich banquet set before him.

The most universal temptation, the one most associated with the Devil through the ages, is the temptation of the flesh. The violence with which Christianity has always attacked sex in any of its more enjoyable aspects (if mildly revelling in masochism), is reflected in the Devil's determined efforts to tempt men and women to indulge themselves in it. (Whether St Paul, for instance, attacked sex because the Devil exhorted men to it, or the Devil concentrated on it because St Paul found it so objectionable, is a moot point.) The ascetics of the early Church went to almost any lengths to escape the fleshly temptations the Devil set before them at every opportunity: they fled to deserts, shut themselves up in caves, mounted the tops of columns. But there was no escape. The records of their temptations are often heart-rending. Poor St Jerome, while camping with the hermits in the desert east of Antioch, was (he later told his friend St Julia Eustochium, a celebrated virgin) tormented often by visions of lubricous dancing-girls. St Victorinus was once almost seduced by the Devil disguised as a beautiful woman. St Francesca Romana received highly unwelcome attentions from one of the most beautiful young men she had ever seen. And St Benedict, driven by the licentiousness of the cities to lonely solitude near Subiaca in Umbria, found himself on one occasion so overcome with lust that he was forced to strip naked and roll in a bramble-bush.

The most ingenious temptations have been devised by Satan. He can make a man (as he made the monk Hero) so puffed up with pride in his own goodness that it can destroy him. He disguised himself as a number of somewhat unmuscular devils, trying to sweep up a pile of leaves, in order to make St Pachomius laugh – for laughter, in the eyes of the Church, can be as irreligious as the enjoyment of sex. Indeed Byron once heard a nonconformist preacher lean from his pulpit to admonish his congregation – 'No hopes for them as *laughs*'!

The Devil often tries to solidify his successes in tempting humans by drawing up legal agreements, generally to be signed in blood – 'a very special sort of juice', as Goethe's Mephistopheles put it. The Faust legend is well known; but there are many others – some involving prominent churchmen. Pope Silvester II (999–1003) was said to have owed his office to a pact with the Devil; Popes John XII (955–64), Benedict IX (1032–59), Gregory VII (1073–85) and Alexander VI (1492–1503) also sold themselves to him for various reasons. In the case of the latter, a Borgia who during his papacy built up an enormous fortune, had many mistresses and organized some of the most elaborate orgies ever recorded, one is not in the least surprised to hear it.

Among the laity, Sir Francis Drake is one of the notabilities whose pact with the Devil was later published: he had sold his soul in exchange for supremacy as an admiral, and was thus able to raise the storm which dispersed the Spanish Armada. Cecco d'Ascolti, a good poet, was burned to death rather earlier (in 1327) for having employed the Devil to teach him astrology.

Many men accepted the Devil's offers in the belief that they could outwit him. They were quite wrong. Anyone proposing a deal with the Devil should take note of the case of a monk whose story is told by the eleventh-century writer Peter Damianus. The monk sold himself to the Devil on condition that the latter should announce his death to him three days in advance – planning, of course, to repent and save his soul during those three days. The Devil, never known to break the form of a contract, did so: but the monk immediately fell into a coma, was unable to make confession and went straight to the hot embrace of his master.

Some men, to whom the Devil has not in the first place appeared, have gone out of their way to summon him. This does not seem to be an extraordinarily difficult procedure: it usually takes place at midnight, perhaps at a point where several roads meet, or in some evocative place such as a bare heath or an empty ruin. It usually involves a circle, or several circles, within which the conjurer places himself for safety. (There are cases of conjurers stupid enough to place so much as a hand outside the circle, and disappearing into the infernal regions. Indeed one young man from Toledo once put out a single finger to receive a gold ring from a luscious dancing-girl. *Zzzzzt!*)

The procedures and invocations used by the conjurers are many and varied, including the familiar *Abracadabra* and its related *Abraxas* – meaningless noise-words with a hypnotic effect, like some of the mantras used in fashionable Eastern religions today. Magicians made up their own books of meaningless incantations, and the magician with his book and his wand became a familiar figure (think of Prospero in *The Tempest*). If he could harness the power of the Devil, he could make himself extremely powerful; but the Devil himself did not care for this procedure, and often got his own back on impertinent humans who attempted to use him for their own purposes. He was usually sufficiently annoyed to make life very uncomfortable for relatively defenceless men.

In modern times diabolism has taken many forms, from the naked caperings of English witches and warlocks in damp coverts in the bracken of Sussex in the cold hours, to the Great Beast Aleister Crowley and his weird and obscene *ménages*, and at its most revolting to Charles Manson and his murderous 'Family' in the United States. It usually seems to have its roots in a sexuality as perverted and in some cases as repressed as any puritan could wish; and it can be said that on the whole the Devil must be proud of his twentieth-century followers.

He has, however, occasionally been defeated – by the Archangel Raphael, for instance, who once indulged in a somewhat undignified tug-of-war for the soul of the eighth-century hermit Barontus, and won. The Virgin, too, has won many disputes with Satan. One or two particularly tenacious saints have even managed to wrestle from the Devil souls he has actually already hauled off to hell. St Gregory freed the soul of the Emperor Trajan by prayer; St Wiborada once regained the soul of a boy of whom he was fond; St Odilo rescued the soul of Pope Benedict IX, though he was in hell strictly as a result of his own agreement with the Devil (who, it seems, can no more hope for justice than for mercy from his great Adversary).

It should be remembered that one or two saints have also actually defeated the Devil in face-to-face conflicts: St Anthony simply by spitting in his face; an Abbot of Cluny by driving him by the sign of the cross into the gentlemen's lavatory there; and St Apollonius by burying him in sand – though history tells us that the Devil on that occasion was disguised as a small Ethiopian gentleman; one must hope there was no mistake.

The Devil's private life in many respects defies examination. There has been much speculation, for instance, about his sexual prowess. The rabbis mention his four wives, and the Emperor of Constantinople's secretary, Michael Psellus, pointed out in the eleventh century that he seems to have all the necessary equipment for procreation. But St Thomas Aquinas, St Bonaventura and others have held that whatever the equipment, the Devil is sterile. This means that in order to procreate, he has to go through the somewhat enervating process of disguising himself as a woman (a *succubus*) and seducing a man; then, having received his sperm, he turns himself into a man (an *incubus*), and seduces and impregnates another woman. The resulting child is not truly the Devil's child, but might

144

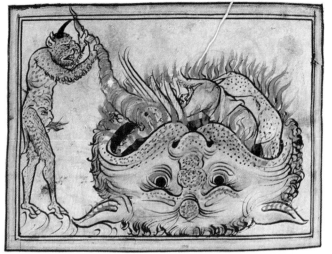

Below: A demon horde advances on the goddess Chandi and Kali. (An Indian painting *c* 1800)
Opposite: A Vajrapani golden vision of Garuda, Vishnu's eagle, and the enemy of all serpents. A Tantric gilded bronze from Nepal

presumably inherit various unpleasant characteristics.

For his own enjoyment, as well as for the pleasure of tempting mankind, the Devil is often found masquerading as *incubus* or *succubus*; but he does seem to prefer to be a man. His poor victims seem to have enjoyed the experience of seduction by the Devil only with some reservations. A girl seduced by him near St Albans in 1440 died after three days, her body bloated and stinking of pollution. Another girl, who was merely kissed by him, went mad, as did a maidservant who only took his hand.

There are indications that the Devil can actually fall in love, and is sometimes successful in gaining the real love of a human woman. Witches are of course his usual solace, though Bishop Alvaro Pelagio, in 1332, said that he had known several nuns who willingly became the Devil's mistress. The Russian poet Lermontov, in a strange and moving poem, *The Demon*, tells how the Devil falls so violently in love with a girl, Tamara, that he actually promises to reform.

Reformation is, however, beyond him. Various early Christian theologians recommended that attempts should be made to convert or save him, but from the sixth century onward it was generally agreed that he was eternally damned – though Hebrews and Mahommedans more charitably believed that he might one day again become a bright angel.

He seems to remain, himself, obdurate. When St Hypatius asked him face to face why he did not repent and rejoin the ranks of the blessed, he quite simply refused to recognize that he had ever sinned – not a very promising start. And in a dispute between himself and Christ, reported by an aural witness, he accused Christ of loving man, a base creature, more than himself, who after all was a creature of angelic nature – a recognizable symptom of supernatural snobbery. He has been known to go to confession at least twice, but has felt unable to submit himself sufficiently to do penance. Milton gives him, in *Paradise Lost,* the dreadful lines

> *Evil, be thou my good; by thee at least*
> *Divided empire with heaven's King I hold,*
> *By thee, and more than half perhaps will*
> *reign . . .*

and Byron's Lucifer, in *Cain,* declares that he will never surrender to the forces of good:

> *Through all eternity*
> *And the unfathomable gulfs of Hades,*
> *And the interminable realms of space,*
> *And the infinity of endless ages,*
> *All, all, will I dispute! And world by world,*
> *And star by star, and universe by universe*
> *Shall tremble in the balance, till the great*
> *Conflict shall cease, if ever it shall cease,*
> *Which it ne'er shall, till He or I be quenched.*

The Devil in several guises

The essence of evil is personified in many national myths by an evil man or beast, often ugly, sometimes victorious, always feared.

Ahriman (Persia)   Prince of demons, creator of death, god of falsehood and darkness; as Ormazd created the good things of the earth, Ahriman created the evil. At first an underworld god, he looks forward to reigning alone after defeating Ormazd.

Apep (Egypt)   Eternal enemy of Ra, Lord of the Sky; a great serpent living in the Nile, at his most dangerous during eclipses.

Chernobog (Balkans)   The black god of evil, and cause of all misfortune.

Chimera (Greece)   A child of Typhon and Echidna, with the body of a goat, the tail of a dragon and the head of a lion, vomiting flames.

Emma-Hoo (Japan)   The ruler of hell, and ferocious judge of sinners.

Hiranyakasipu (India)   A demon-king who proclaimed himself master of the universe.

Kali (India)   One of the ten manifestations of Siva's wife: a dark woman with long hair and four arms, wearing two corpses as earrings and a necklace of human skulls.

Loki (Scandinavia)   A handsome fire-demon, servant of the Teutonic gods, utterly untrustworthy; a great liar who eventually brought about his masters' destruction.

Letan (Syria and Palestine)   The biblical Leviathan, the primeval serpent, the Torturous One with seven heads.

Midgard (Germany)   A huge reptile whose coils encircle the world.

Ngurvilu (Chile)   A wild-cat water-god, with a claw on the end of his tail.

Set (Egypt)   Osiris' red-haired evil brother and murderer; god of the unclean, with the head of a beast and a forked tail.

Tezcatlipoca (Mexico)   A sun-god and racial enemy of Quetzalcoatl, with a bear's face, yellow and black, and bells on his ankles. The cause of all intrigue and war.

Tuoni (Finland)   With his wife Tuonetar, the ruler of the underworld, Tuonela; the father of Loviatar, a girl of unspeakable ugliness, and source of all evil.

Typhoeus (Greece)   A mountain-sized god with a hundred dragons' heads breathing fire, thighs covered with vipers, who once subdued the gods – even Zeus; but finally was vanquished by the latter.

Vritra (India)   A demon created to fight the Brahman gods.

An
IMMORTAL BESTIARY

It is not too difficult to understand why animals have taken their place in the ranks of the immortals. Their very silence is mysterious – they are beings who live among, or at least in the same world as, men; who are evidently creatures of understanding and intelligence; yet they choose to remain silent, uncommunicative. Looking into the eyes of a cat, even modern man can imagine some depth of knowledge, some enigma; no wonder the Egyptians venerated them so profoundly that to kill one, even accidentally, was to deserve death. Veneration for the cat in ancient Egypt reached an intense pitch. At a time when it was vital to maintain good relations with Egypt, a visiting Roman (Diodorus reports) killed one of the sacred animals. Despite his Roman citizenship and despite the pleas of Egyptian politicians, the mob fell upon his house, sacked it and killed him. Herodotus notes that when a house caught fire, the first and most important task was to rescue any cat it contained; then attention could be turned to human life and property.

The Egyptian goddess most intimately connected with the cat was Bast, a cat-headed woman from Bubastis, in Lower Egypt, to whose elegant festivals in the fourth century BC hundreds of thousands of worshippers would journey. There was a fine trade in small cat-statuettes, and mummified cats were lovingly buried in the goddess's sanctuary.

Though European societies rarely achieved the superb show of Bast's ceremonies, let alone the artistry of the Egyptian cat-carvings, the animal retained its hold on human imagination. In the East, and in West Africa, the souls of the dead were often believed to pass into the body of a cat, or to be borne away by one. In the West, cats have not been so dignified – despite the Italian legend that a cat gave birth to kittens beneath Christ's manger. By far the closest association of supernatural and feline powers has been, traditionally, in witchcraft.

Almost every witch, in the dark days of the persecutions, had her cat: a lonely old woman could scarcely afford to keep one in the house, for fear of suspicion. But even the cat-in-the-street was a creature to treat with care: Somerset people never discussed secrets in front of one – it was too likely to be a witch in disguise. Cats born in May were particularly suspect, for that was a month associated with the spirits of the dead, and May kittens were best drowned before they could grow up and do any harm.

Cats are particularly sensitive to ghosts. Unlike dogs, which mistrust spirits, cats are always pleased to see them, and purr welcomingly at their appearance. They can, however, bring good luck – a cat sneezing near a bride on her wedding day forecasts a happy marriage. Black cats on the whole are lucky (white cats less so) and they are useful as meteorologists, forecasting wind by scratching the carpet, rain by washing their ears.

The Englishman's traditional love of dogs cannot have had its origins in myth, for the dog has always had a rather unpleasant mythical reputation, often being associated with evil and disaster – even in the British Isles, where Black Shuck strides alone through the lanes of East Anglia, the size of a calf and with saucer-eyes blazing green in the dark, precursor of ill-fortune. In Wales, the Dog of Darkness, Gwyllgi, is even larger, paralysing humans with the terror of his weird howl, and pole-axing them with one glance from his eyes. The Mauthe Dog or Moddey Dhoo, of the Isle of Man, is another famous spectral hound, most often seen at Peel Castle, where it used to stand guard, terrifying both those who kept the castle and those who attacked it.

Elsewhere, dogs of hell appear in the legends of many countries; they manifest themselves as packs of death-hounds which run baying through the skies of northern Europe in a ghastly wild hunt. The Welsh Cwn Annwn are dogs of hell, predicting death for those who see them. A more pleasantly useful creature is the Shony Dog, of Cornwall, which announces the coming of storms, thus saving fishermen from death and destruction on the rocky shores. The dog's association with mortality is a pervasive one: the Ugandan Nandi dislike and suspect dogs because it was a dog who, in their eyes, brought death into the world: he had been told to announce to man his immortality, but the Nandi tribesmen treated him disrespectfully, making him eat his meals sitting on a stool like a human, and laughing at him. Irritated beyond bearing, he announced: 'All men shall die – only the moon shall be reborn.' And so indeed it was.

In Norse mythology there is an unpleasant, blood-spashed creature called Garmr, which watches over the House of the Dead, and will fight the gods when hell's wolves devour the sun and moon. Hell's wolves (and wolf legends often seem to run parallel to those of dogs) seem to spend most of

Dragons, 'most greatest of all serpents' according to
Bartholomew Anglicus, guard the Machendranath Temple at
Katmandu

appease him, for he developed a spiteful tendency to bite new arrivals. One cannot help feeling that *three* honey-cakes would have been a better premium.

That other warmly domesticated animal the horse has always had a close relationship with man, even guiding him (the Celts believed) to the realms of the dead. Its psychic powers are like those of cat and dog, highly developed, and it is said like the cat to be able to see spirits. St Columba surely owned a remarkable horse, which foresaw its master's death and wept bitterly at the prospect. Less friendly were the wild horses that martyred three other saints – St Anastasius, St Hippolytus and St Quirinus.

There were certain horse-gods and goddesses, or immortals with horses' heads, in ancient times. The dramatic chalk figures of horses carved into hillsides in England two thousand or more years ago show the relationship to the cult of Epona, a horse-goddess who in Gaul is shown riding a horse, but later seems actually to have become one. Lady

their time chasing the sun and moon, like gigantic balls; and when they catch them the mightiest of them will devour the sun, and bring about the end of the world. In Wales, it has long been traditional for farmers not to mention wolves during the twelve days of Christmas, for fear of bad luck. One kindly wolf does much to redeem the others: it was a she-wolf which suckled Romulus and Remus, the founders of Rome.

The East is not lacking in unpleasant immortal dogs: less surprisingly, as the canine/human relationship is less close in the Orient. In both Buddhism and Brahmanism there are hells full of dogs, the torturers of human souls – though in China, the Celestial Dog, T'ien-kou, helps his master Ehr-lang to drive away evil spirits from the palace of the August Personage of Jade.

The strongest link in the chain of relationship between dog and death was the Greek Cerberus, the guard-dog of Hades. His three heads represented the past, present and future, and he had a serpent for a tail with which he would greet newcomers to hell. As it was Cerberus' job to discourage (by tearing to pieces) those who wished to leave, he constantly sat facing inwards or downwards, ready to grab potential escapers. Hercules managed to overcome him in his Twelfth Labour, and it was considered good insurance for humans to place a honey-cake in their coffin as a pleasant morsel to

Horse-head, in Chinese mythology, was promised by her mother in marriage to the man who was able to recover her father from the pirates who had kidnapped him. The horse, in love with his mistress, did so; but was killed by his ungrateful master and skinned. It was the skin which wrapped itself around the girl and carried her off. In the Chinese hell, Ma-mien, or Horse-face, is one of the two messengers sent to bear a man's soul to the lower world.

In almost every ancient superstition, the sun was drawn across the sky by eternal horses. Dag, the Norse god of day, was escorted by a marvellous white horse called Shining Mane, while Mani, the moon-goddess, drove Alsvidur, the All Swift. Diana, Thor and Helion all maintained their own chariots and horses; Odin's horse, for additional swiftness and dexterity, had eight hooves.

A war-horse was often made immortal by sacrifice at the death of its warrior-master, so that it could

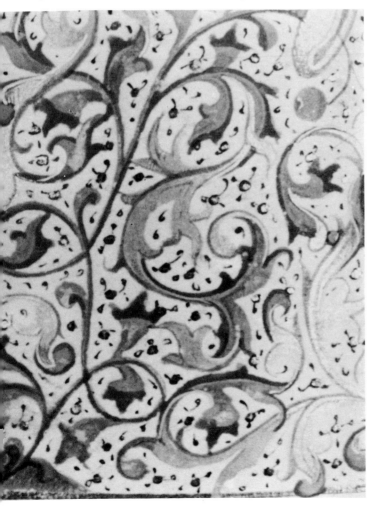

share his life in the afterworld – a practice continued in central Asia until this century. Until the eighteenth century, in western Europe, horses were burned alive as a nauseating insurance against the theft of other animals or their death from disease.

There are two theories about the origin of Pegasus, the most famous of winged horses. One was that he was a son of Poseidon, commander of the seas; the other that he was made from the drops of blood which fell from the monster Medusa's head as Perseus flew off with it. Pegasus was ridden by Bellerophon when he slew the Chimera; later, he tried to ride him to heaven, but fell off and was killed. Pegasus was the symbol of inspiration, and it was he who, with a single blow of his hoof, opened the fountain of Hippocrene on Mount Olympus, where the poets drink.

The feeling of oneness between man and horse is marvellously symbolized in one of the most delightful of all imaginary species, the Centaur. The first centaurs were the offspring of Ixion, a king of Thessaly, and a cloud which Zeus had made in the shape of a goddess. Another theory asserts that centaurs were the result of a Greek hero with a serpent's tail, Centaurus, mating with the mares of Magnesium. But horse-riding was unknown to the Greeks of the Homeric period, and one may conjecture that the first Scythian horsemen they met really seemed to be dual creatures of the centaur kind. At all events they are exceptionally appealing and handsome creatures, and there is no doubt which side one is on when looking at the battle between them and their human attackers depicted in the Elgin marbles.

In Christian iconography, centaurs sometimes appear as a symbol of sensuality. The best-known centaur was probably Cheiron, king of his species and a friend of Hercules, who taught Achilles and Aesculapius hunting, music and the arts of war. When Hercules accidentally shot him with a poisoned arrow, he surrendered his immortality to Prometheus, to avoid everlasting agony; and Zeus placed him among the stars, where he is still to be seen as the constellation Sagittarius.

In Sumerian legend, Cheiron is paralleled by Hes Bani, half-man, half-bull, also celebrated for his wisdom. Other creatures provide variations on the theme of duality: from the Scythian Ipopodes, with only the legs and hooves of horses, to the onocentaurs, presumably less intelligent, being half-man, half-ass. A beguilingly independent beast, the onocentaur placed so much importance on his freedom that he would rather starve to death than sacrifice it.

The Far East has its own centaur, the Celestial Horse of China, with fleshy wings with which it can fly, though in appearance it resembles a white dog with a black head. Mohammed's milk-white flying steed, Al Borak, used to carry his master on his nightly journeys to the seven heavens, with a stride so vast that it could reach to the furthest range of human sight. He has, in Eastern paintings, a man's face, ass's ears, a horse's body and the plumage of a peacock.

Even more hybrid is the hippogriph, produced by mating a horse with a griffin. Since the griffin is a cross between an eagle and a lion, it may be conjectured that the hippogriph is a rather rare creature.

Unlike the horse, which has taken some strange forms in its mythical history, the bull always seems to remain recognizably a bull. Its legends often have passionate and lusty overtones, characteristics which are among those attributed to subjects of the second sign of the zodiac, Taurus. The Milk White Bull is a favourite immortal of myth: Siva, the Hindu god, rode one, and has his jovial moments. It was in the guise of a white bull that the immortal Jove presented himself to the young and beautiful Europa, to seduce her.

But the paramount bull story reaches over two generations. Pasiphae, Queen of Crete, developed a furious passion for a white bull brought from the sea by Neptune. The result of their dynamic union was the Minotaur, half-man, half-bull. He lived in a specially designed labyrinth, and was fed annually upon seven Athenian men and maidens. He was eventually slain by Theseus, who won the love of the King of Crete's daughter, Ariadne. She had told Theseus how to slay the beast, and gave him a skein of thread with which he could retrace his footsteps through the maze.

It seems likely that the Minotaur was a rather late and clumsy version of a much older legend. Certainly the bull has been portrayed in very early art: his connection with the ancient Egyptians and their preoccupation with life after death certainly predates Greece.

Enlil, the bull-god of Sumeria in the third millennium BC, was the great god of fertility, from whom a whole nation drew its life-force when the Babylonians made him one with their god Marduk. He lived in the Great Mountains of the East, dispensing both good and evil, and his consort Belit nourished with her milk the human heroes who were set aside to become kings.

In Egypt, the black bull Apis was worshipped at Memphis as the reincarnation of Ptah, protector of artists and artisans, one of the most important of the

An Indian lady on friendly terms with a bull, often the symbol
of male potency

An asp could rot away a man with a single bite; while a charmer could lull it. It could (as below) resist by stopping one ear with its tail, and placing the other to the ground make itself stone-deaf

gods. Recognized at his birth by the white triangle on his forehead, the crescent moon on his right flank, and other signs, the fortunate animal spent an idyllic life lolloping about his own temple forecourt (each movement foretelling a future event), until he died of old age – though at least two sacred bulls were assassinated by Egypt's enemies, and were mourned inconsolably until the discovery of their successors. At Saqqara was a huge sepulchre where the sacred bulls, mummified and carefully buried, lay for eternity – or at least until 1850, when they were discovered and disturbed by archaeologists.

The cow, with her abundance of milk, is of course mainly a symbol of plenitude and fertility: the Egyptian goddess Hathor, mother of the sun-god, was often represented as a cow, as was Nut, goddess of the sky. On the whole, the mild and gentle cow seems in mythology to have retained those pleasant, somewhat melancholy qualities, though the Dun Cow of Warwick lost her patience on one occasion. She originally travelled from Shropshire (in the tenth century) in order to supply milk to the local giants in a neighbouring county. She was a large beast and had the reputation that her supply of milk was endless. An unpleasant old woman doubted the

story, and took a sieve to her to see if this was true. The cow was furious, broke loose and wandered into Warwickshire, where she was slain by Guy of Warwick. The latter, evidently, was a splenetic gentleman with a penchant for killing strange beasts; he had already disposed of two monsters, a Northumberland dragon and two visiting Danish giants.

One of the most delightful cow legends is from Scandinavia, where a cow called Authumia was fashioned from condensing frost during the creation of the world, her milk nourishing the first being, Ymir the Giant. When she licked the salty ice-blocks, they formed themselves into the ancestors of the gods.

In spite of the fact that most cow legends are gentle by nature – none more charming than the French one which says that a cow's breath is sweet because it warmed the infant Jesus in the manger – there are also connections between cows and death. In the British Isles it was said that a cow breaking into someone's garden was a death-omen. And in Anglo-Saxon England, and more recently in Scandinavia and Germany, a cow would accompany a coffin on its way to church. The Hindu cow (sacred and not to be killed) had the kindly attribute that if a person died while holding on to its tail, it would guide him safely through the other world. The two stories meet: accompanying the coffin, the cow acted as a guide. Perhaps the cow's milk symbolized sustenance for the journey: as it was our first food in this world, perhaps it should also be our first food in the next.

It was not, of course, only domesticated animals, or even those capable of a certain amount of domesticity, that were regarded as worthy of immortality. The lion, for instance, with its innate dignity, has always been associated with the idea of royalty, and became the symbol of goddesses like the Greek Artemis and the Egyptian Sekhmet, goddess of war and battle, as well as of human regality. In the Congo, lions possess the souls of great dead chiefs (though elsewhere in Africa – among the Ngonis, for instance – any warrior may look forward to that metamorphosis).

The lioness is a creature of great passion, making love with whoever or whatever comes her way. A curious habit of the lion is to couple with the ant, or so scholars of the Dark Ages believed, declining to describe the mechanics of the affair. The resulting creature, the ant-lion, is a lion in front and an ant at the back. There is reference to this creature in the Book of Job, and early writers seem to have accepted it without question. However, they did see that it would have had some difficulty in surviving, since its front half was carnivorous and its rear half vegetarian. In fact, its presence in the Bible was the result of a simple mistranslation.

The wolf, much feared in medieval times, is usually, in his immortal guise, a rather unpleasant figure: the goddess Hecate can become a wolf, and in Scandinavia one of Loki's three children is a wolf. Upuaut, the wolf-headed god of Egypt, pilots the sun's boat as it passes through the dark underworld. The jackal and hyena also take their place in the hierarchy: the hyena has a stone in its eye in which a man may see his future – though with care, for if the hyena can walk around him three times, he will be paralysed. The hyena has the property of being both male and female, in alternate years, and is capable of some unpleasant deceptions – by imitating the sound of a man vomiting, it can bring humans to offer help, when they will be attacked and killed. It most enjoys living in vaults and crypts, where it devours human corpses.

The jackal is less actively unpleasant than shrewd and cunning. Often, no doubt because of its habits as a scavenger, it is associated with death, as in Egypt, where, as the jackal-headed Anubis, it guarded cemeteries and escorted the dead to the presence of Osiris.

These were animals who were regarded as personifying gods, or even as containing the souls of gods. Even more fascinating and astonishing are the other creatures – the true immortals, if you like – whose immortality is completely invulnerable because they do not exist. Perhaps the most charming of these is the unicorn.

As far as one can gather, the first description of the unicorn was made by the Greek historian Ctesias of Cnidos, who in the fourth century BC wrote of 'certain wild asses' with white bodies, dark red heads, dark blue eyes, and 'a horn on the forehead which is about a foot and a half in length'. They were of amazing fleetness, and would undoubtedly be extremely difficult to capture. Travellers disagreed about the nature of the unicorn: one described it as extremely fierce, another as excessively mild and nervous. Either of these characteristics would have contributed to the difficulties of hunting it. But in medieval times an almost infallible means of snaring the unicorn was discovered, hinging on its predeliction for young virgins. The Abbess Hildegard pointed out in a handbook written in the twelfth century that the beast would gaze adoringly at a pure girl who had never been led astray, especially if she were naked. And a century later, a German ecclesiastic avowed that, meeting such a girl, the creature would be so awed that it would quietly lay its head in her lap.

The glow of gratification on the faces of some of the virgins in early paintings as they contemplate the horn on the head of the unicorn reclining in their laps, seems to indicate post-coital relaxation; and the marvellously aphrodisiac qualities of powdered unicorn-horn contribute to the sexual elements of the story. Most druggists in the Middle Ages kept a stock of powdered horn, which was good for curing diarrhoea as well as impotence. Complete horns were used as drinking vessels, and were extremely valuable – one kept at Windsor Castle in the sixteenth century was valued at £10,000.

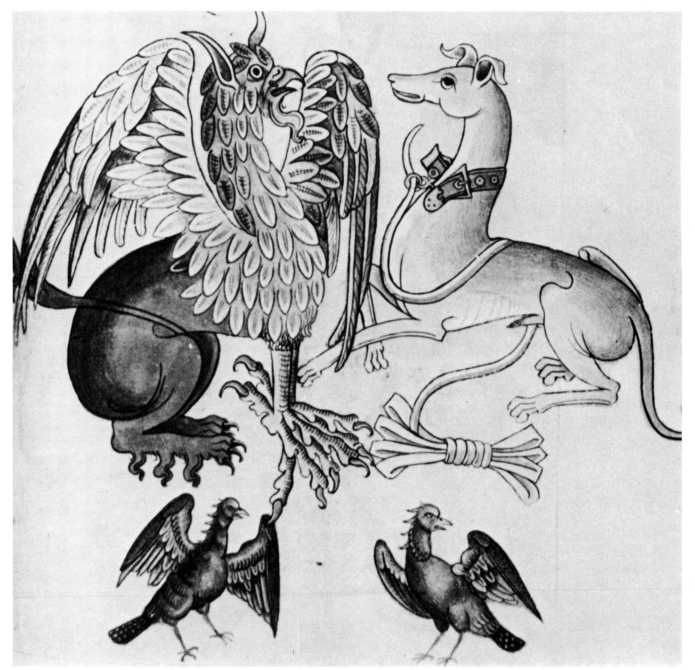

Fierce though the unicorn could undoubtedly be
(however mild in the presence of a naked virgin –
Aelian, in the second century BC, described its
violence to its own species, male and female, and
Isadore of Seville spoke of it as 'mortall enimy to the
Oelphant') the basilisk probably outdid it. Pliny
described the basilisk as a snake which carried itself
proudly erect and was so poisonous that if you
pierced it with a spear, the poison, like an electric
current, ran straight up the spear into your arm. It
could kill a man by a simple glance of its eye, or by
the smell of its sweat, and could set fire even to
stones by breathing on them. The former attribute
had its dangers, for – as with Medusa – a mirror
could be its downfall: glimpsing its own piercing
gaze, it would be paralysed. Another means of
killing the basilisk was to produce an ordinary
domestic cockerel, whose crow for some reason
threw the poisonous beast into a fit. Travellers
crossing North African deserts, infested with
basilisks, rarely set out without a good supply of
cockerels.

The connection between snake-basilisks and cocks had a strange result, for by the Middle Ages travellers were describing a new kind of basilisk: with a serpent's rear and a cock's head, sometimes called a basilicoc, and later a cockatrice, which was believed to be born from the immeasurably tough egg of a cockerel, hatched by a toad. A cockatrice was hatched in the cellars of Wherwell Priory, Hampshire, in 1538, and was killed by a Mr Green after it had devoured several local people. A portrait of the beast, once a weathercock on Wherwell Church, is now in Andover Museum.

In the procession of strange beasts which parades through the bestiaries, the unicorn and basilisk lead some very odd beings indeed. Among these is the eale, with an elephant's tail and boar's head, and two horns which can be pointed independently in any direction – a great advantage in a fight. Then comes the centichora, an Indian animal with a body like a

A griffin making off with a pig. From an English bestiary, *c* 1200
Overleaf: A phoenix in the midst of regenerating flames. From a thirteenth-century bestiary

lion, the legs and feet of a horse, huge ears in place of teeth (so the descriptions say), and again, long, swivelling, sharp horns. One of the few animals which could defeat a centichora was the basilisk, which unsportingly and puzzlingly poisoned it when it was asleep.

The cantoblepas is perhaps a slightly less vicious beast, though only just. With a thick mane falling over its eyes like the hair of some all-in wrestler, it feeds on poisonous herbs, which make its breath fatal to man. The griffin depends on no such subtlety for its victories, but simply on the strength of its claws, each of which is large enough to be used as a drinking-horn. Bartholomew Anglicus described it as 'like to the lion in all parts of the body, and to the eagle only in the head and wings'. It is strong enough to carry away an animal in its claws, and in its narrow cave precious stones make a comfortable bed.

Few of these fabulous creatures are sufficiently attractive, one would have thought, to seduce even the most sensual human being; yet the presence of half-human beasts in the mythology of the world seems to indicate that a coupling of man and monster must sometimes have taken place. Centaurs have already been mentioned: but there are other strange beings whose reality was for a while totally accepted.

There are enough portraits of satyrs to provide a convincing body of evidence that they were once common. The handsome, sly, boyish faces, full of charm, are crowned by a pair of horns, while goatish thighs, hooves and tail complete the picture. One of the sexiest of all immortals, the satyr particularly lusted after human women, as Ephemur Car, an early traveller, recounts:

Being perceived by the mariners to run to the ships, and lay hold on the women that were in them, the shipmen for fear took one of the barbarian women and set her on the land among them, whom in most odious and filthy manner they abused, not only in that part that nature hath ordained, but over the whole body most libidinously, whereby they found them to be very brute beasts.

St Anthony (or perhaps St Paul the Hermit – accounts vary) once met a satyr in the deserts of Egypt, who when questioned replied: 'I am a creature that Christ made deadly, and in this desert 163

I dwell and go for to get my sustenance.' One wonders how he was able to answer the good saint's questions, since, unlike the usual satyr, he was man from the navel downwards, and goat above the waist.

The martichoras was first seen, or at least first described, by the Greek Ctesias. It has a sort of human face, though with three rows of teeth, a hairy body like a lion's, a scorpion's tail which could fire poisoned quills at an attacker, and a voice (Aristotle said) rather like the combination of a trumpet and a reed-pipe.

These creatures used force or poison to attack men. The Lamia attracted him, or so it is reported, by sexuality, able as she was to transform herself into a beautiful woman – not unlike the gorgon of Perseus' story (able to slay with a glance of a basilisk eye), or the Scottish Glaistig, which sucked the blood of any young man who danced with it while it was in a human girl's skin.

Local variations on the monster theme can be found all over the world, wherever the sudden disappearance or death of men or beasts prompts them, and there are various dark shadows lurking in various regions of the British Isles. In the caves of Wales, afancs (Welsh centaurs) live. One, which fell in love with a local girl at Conway, was actually caught, bound with ropes and exiled to the top of Snowdon. Missing sheep in Wales have usually fallen victim to the Llamigan-y-dur, shaped like a huge toad, and with wings and a tail; it lives in deep freshwater pools. Missing Scottish sheep have probably fallen prey to the boobrie, a vast duck living in the sea-lochs of Argyll – though the culprit may after all have been the fearful nuckelavee, a skinless barrel of a beast whose awful interior may be seen as through transparent plastic.

The immortal zoo with all its real and imaginary characters has survived too long to be neglected. We may now smile at the readiness of the medieval traveller to accept stories of centichores or cantoblepas, but how much stranger in shape is the elephant? We may feel a pang of nostalgia for the unicorn; but motorists have reported seeing Black Schuk as it makes its way across the deserted moorlands of East Anglia. . . .

The IMMORTAL UN-DEAD

Vampires

The *Oxford English Dictionary* is quite unequivocal: *vampire* – 'a preternatural being of a malignant nature (in the original and usual form of the belief, a reanimated corpse), supposed to seek nourishment, or do harm, by sucking the blood of sleeping persons. . . .' Since blood is so vitally associated with life and the body's welfare, it is not surprising that it has been associated with religious rituals, some of them (like those of the Aztecs) extremely unpleasant. Granted the notion that a dead man might continue to walk – as a potentially immortal 'un-dead' – it would be blood, of course, that he would need; fresh blood, and plenty of it. And where would he get it but from the veins of a healthy living person? Enlarge the situation to ensure that it is the blood of a beautiful young girl or a handsome, virile young man that is most efficacious in keeping the un-dead alive, and you have prepared the stage for the vampire at his most active.

Though it was the author Bram Stoker in his novel *Dracula* (and in its subsequent stage and screen adaptations) who was mainly instrumental in making the vampire famous in the modern literature of horror, the legend itself originated long before 1897, when the novel was first published. In ancient Greece there was a belief that, if a dog or cat jumped over a corpse, it might be reanimated as a vampire; and various precautions were taken to deter the vampires which already existed from making their way into the houses of the genuinely alive. Hedges of brambles would be placed before the doors, and mustard-seed spread there, in the belief that any visiting vampire would either become inextricably entangled, or at least would feel compelled to pause and count the mustard-seed, giving the inhabitants time to escape. Similar legends and superstitions were recorded in China and the East.

But it was in eastern Europe that the legend of

"Well, it may be so." cried the blacksmith, "but still it's good advice, and as I said before it comes to this—is we to be afraid ot lay down in our beds at night, or isn't we?"

Before any reply could be made to this interrogatory, the old clock that was in the public-house parlour struck the hour of eleven, and another peal of thunder seemed to be answering to the tinkling sounds.

"It's a rough night," said one, "I thought there would be a storm before morning by the look of the sun at setting—it went down with a strange fiery redness behind a bank of clouds. I move for going home."

"Who talks of going home," cried the blacksmith, "when vampires are abroad? hasn't old Timothy said, that a stormy night was the very one to settle the thing in."

"No," cried another, "he did not say night at all."

"I don't care whether he said night or day; I've made up my mind to do something; there's no doubt about it but that a vampyre is about the old church. Who'll come with me and ferret it out? it will be good service done to everybody's fireside."

A great many efforts were made to get him to say more, particularly with reference to the case under consideration, as being no common one, but the octogenarian had made his effort, and he only replied to the remonstrances of those who, alternately by coaxing and bullying, strove to get information from him, by a vacant stare.

"It's of no use," said the butcher, "you'll get nothing more now from old Timothy; he's done up now, that's quite clear, and ten to one if the excitement of to-night won't go a good way towards slaughtering him before his time."

No. 1.]   Nos. 2, 3 and 4 are Presented, Gratis, with this No.   [Price 1d.

VARNEY THE VAMPIRE. OR THE FEAST OF BLOOD

A ROMANCE OF EXCITING INTEREST.

BY THE AUTHOR OF
"GRACE RIVERS; OR, THE MERCHANT'S DAUGHTER."

LONDON: E. LLOYD, SALISBURY-SQUARE, AND ALL BOOKSELLERS.

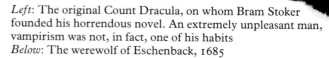

Left: The original Count Dracula, on whom Bram Stoker founded his horrendous novel. An extremely unpleasant man, vampirism was not, in fact, one of his habits
Below: The werewolf of Eschenback, 1685

himself into a bat. (The vampire bat, a legend in Europe, is of course a reality in South America, Java and Sumatra; it too hypnotizes its victims before sucking their blood.)

As to dealing with a vampire once he had been recognized, there were several means. For protection, there was the garlic and the cross, or a ring of holy water from within which one could shoot him with a silver bullet, pierce his breast with a pick, or strike his head clean off with one blow. Caught alive, he could be hanged, and a stake driven through his heart. Or, his head removed, he could be burned, and would grow visibly older in the flames until at last only wizened skin and bones remained.

That kind of detail abounded, and bolstered the legend. But there was other evidence. Sometimes, when the coffins of suspected vampires were opened, the bodies would be found twisted into strange attitudes, or, instead of showing symptoms of decay, would be fresh-faced and plump, grinning diabolically, or with their eyes wide open and staring. It would take only one or two cases of tragic premature burial to account for the many stories which circulated. More convincingly still, there were eye-witness descriptions of vampires. They

vampirism grew to its full height – particularly in Transylvania, a province nipped between the Carpathians and the Transylvanian Alps, where Romanians, Hungarians and Germans mingled to make up a race, the Magyars, particularly volatile and imaginative in the nurturing of myth. Like the werewolf, the *nosferatu* or vampire was held in peculiar horror: not only because of an instinctive fear of a creature which could come quietly, at night, to suck the lifeblood from your veins without so much as disturbing your slumber, but because a body of circumstantial rumour built up to give the vampire a spurious but complex verisimilitude.

The vampire was known to hate garlic, to shrink from a crucifix, to be unable to cross water, to show no image in a mirror. One smelt his approach: a stench of the charnel-house hung about him; his long, dirty fingernails were blackened by his digging himself in and out of the coffin in which he slept during the day, and marked him out – as did his ashen-white face and piercing black eyes (capable of hypnotism). And of course there were the long, white teeth ready to puncture the skin of the victim's throat. He was capable too of turning were never seen at work – at least not by their victims, lulled into deep sleep. The only sign they showed of the fiend's attentions was a wasting sickness, under which they grew weaker and weaker, paler and paler, until eventually, their blood almost drained, they would be forced to become vampires themselves, would be infected with the germ of immortality and join the ranks of the un-dead. (A dead man or woman suspected of having died of 'the vampire's kiss' would often be buried with a piece of the consecrated host on their chest, to ensure that they did not become *un-dead*.)

But there were some convincing documents of face-to-face encounters, nevertheless. One of the most graphic was signed by three army surgeons, a lieutenant-colonel and a sub-lieutenant, who investigated a case reported at Meduegna, near Belgrade, in the eighteenth century. In 1727 a young man called Arnold Paole had retired from army service to settle down as a smallholder near Meduegna. A pleasant enough young man, he nevertheless had an air of melancholy about him, and when he became engaged to a neighbour's daughter he was persuaded to tell her the reason for his depression. It seems that when he was on army service in Greece, he had been in contact with one of the un-dead, and though he did not believe that he

had suffered any ill, the experience haunted him. Shortly after this revelation, Paole died after a fall from a wagon, and was buried in Meduegna churchyard. Within a month, there were reports that he had been seen at night in the village; the rumour was that he had become a vampire.

The village decided that Paole's body should be disinterred, and the army was invited to assist. A commission consisting of two officers, three army surgeons, with a drummer-boy to carry their instruments, and some other military men, gathered one cold dawn in the churchyard with local dignitaries. An eye-witness described how Paole's coffin was uncovered, and the lid knocked off: 'It was seen that the corpse had moved to one side, the jaws gaped wide open, and the blue lips were moist with new blood which had trickled in a thin stream from the corner of the mouth. All unafraid, the old sexton caught the body and twisted it straight. "So," he cried, "you have not wiped your mouth since last night's work!"' Pausing only to drag away the body of the drummer-boy, who not surprisingly had fainted, the surgeons scattered garlic over the remains and drove a stake through the body – whereupon a fountain of blood spouted from the wound, and there was a piercing scream.

A commission of inquiry was held in the same village a few years later, after another outbreak of vampirism. The commission ordered the disinterment of the body of a girl who had died three months earlier, after confessing to having anointed herself with the blood of a vampire. The body was uncorrupted, the chest full of fresh blood and the viscera healthy. There were clean new skin and nails on the hands and feet. Several other bodies were found to be in 'a healthy and plump condition', while the bodies of others who had died at the same time were decomposed. The account may be 'fact' but it reads like fiction, and the fictional literature of vampirism is extensive. Dr John William Polidori, Byron's emotionally unbalanced physician (who eventually went mad) was first in the field with *The Vampyre*, a novel based on his most famous patient's idea, and published in 1819. It went into a great many editions, and was adapted for the Paris stage (Alexandre Dumas much enjoyed it, and was inspired to write his own play on the same theme). Thomas Preskett Prest, an extremely prolific and exceptionally untalented novelist, published *Varney the Vampire* in 1847. It was an enormous success, its opening chapter (an orgasm of melodramatic Grand

169

Below: 'An exact representation of the wild beast now in France, in the act of devouring a young woman.' News-sheet, *c* 1660
Opposite: *A Witches' Sabbath*, by Franz Francken (*c* 1544–1616)

Guignol) describing the vampire's attack on a beautiful maiden asleep in a dark Elizabethan bedchamber: 'The glassy, horrible eyes of the figure ran over that angelic form with a hideous satisfaction – horrible profanation. He dragged her head to the bed's edge. He forced it back by the long hair still entwined in his grasp. With a plunge he seized her neck in his fang-like teeth – a gush of blood, and a hideous sucking noise followed. The girl had swooned – and the vampire was at his hideous repast!'

Then, in 1897, cane *Dracula*, the most notorious vampire novel of all, still splendidly readable. It was written by Bram Stoker, sometime business manager to the actor Sir Henry Irving, later to be a professor of English literature. A splendid example of the horror story *genre*, not surprisingly it caught the public imagination, and still retains it, together with innumerable weaker imitations. If the vampire, like the gods, is dead to most modern men, it certainly lives (as they do) in legend and literature.

Witches

Witches and warlocks – men or women who attempt to tap the power of some evil deity – considerably predate Christianity. Indeed their activity in Europe seems to have originated in paleolithic times, when peasants who lived as simple farmers worshipped a horned god symbolic of the fertility of cattle, sheep, goats or deer. His faint shadow grew into the Christian Devil, with horns and tail. Probably a local 'priest' wearing an animal's head and skin impersonated this diety.

The history of witchcraft is permeated with sexuality, which is one reason why it was so hated by the early Church. But by the Christian age the idea of witchcraft was too strongly established to be easily discounted. In the earliest times (there are illustrations of witchcraft on the walls of paleolithic caves at Altamira in Spain and Ariège in France) the magic was on the whole 'good', the rites held at Candlemas, May Eve, Lammas and November Eve supposedly promoting fertility among cattle and humans alike. However, those who became especially adept in magic gained the reputation of being able, also, by reversing the procedure in some way, to bring about sterility and death.

Witches attached themselves to religion after religion – to the worship of Jupiter and Odin, and then of Christ – though they never put themselves forward as the 'priests' of those religions: what they provided was, in a way, an antidote to them. The ruling classes of a country supported a particular religion. The witches showed how the humble people of the same country could have their own power, milked from the evil powers of that same religion; for if nobles worshipped Odin, Odin's opponents (the witches' friends) must be on the side of the peasants.

Nonconformists and heretics were often accounted witches throughout the Christian era. King William Rufus of England was thought a warlock, and so was the wicked Gilles de Rais (or Retz), patron of Joan of Arc, herself branded as a witch. By the time of the Reformation, accusations of witchcraft were a useful means of stigmatizing political plotters. 'Witches' formed secret societies, or covens, generally speaking with thirteen members, and usually led by a man, though both men and women could belong to them. Sometimes they may have been seriously occupied with the occult; more usually, they were either politically orientated, or (as one suspects of twentieth-century witches) emotionally disturbed.

An illustration from a sixteenth-century *Treatise on Witchcraft*: broomsticks, lighted candles and a goat play their part in ritual, while fully-fledged witches ride in the background

In England there were laws against witches from the time of King Canute (1000–36). Both ecclesiastical and secular courts had power to try people for witchcraft, and the Church exercised those powers until 1542, when it became a common felony. From the Middle Ages until the eighteenth century trials for witchcraft provide copious, fascinating and tragic reading. The earliest reported trial in England before a secular court was in 1324, that of the famous Dame Alice Kyteler. But it was in the seventeenth century that witchcraft became, according to court records, an epidemic: over 200 people were convicted of witchcraft in the Home Counties of England alone between 1558 and 1736.

The history of witchcraft in Europe mirrors in a most interesting way the social history of the various countries. In England for instance there were few accusations that witches had actually been in direct touch with the Devil, as was common in some parts of Europe. Nor were there so many accusations concerned with flying on broomsticks or metamorphoses into animals. Most English witches were accused of damaging their neighbours' property – and English law has always been much concerned with the protection of property. To accuse a neighbour of being a witch was an all too easy way of punishing him or her for any slight, for it was almost impossible for an accused person to escape conviction, so complex were the laws on the subject. This led to many, often tragic, cases – perhaps the most notorious being the trials at Salem, north of Boston, Massachusetts, where in 1692 a few hysterical girls made accusations which resulted in the trial of many innocent members of the community. Nineteen people were hanged, and one – Giles Corey, who had accused his wife of witchcraft, but then was himself accused of being a wizard – refused to plead, and was pressed to death beneath a pile of stones. Perhaps the bestknown of the Salem 'witches' was Sarah Good, a malicious and deceitful old woman who died cursing the clergymen who, on the gallows, called on her to confess. He is said to have died himself as she prophesied, choking in his own blood, years later.

Witchcraft records reveal the depths to which human nature can sink when religious hysteria and sexual tension gain their hold: Henry Kramer's and James Sprenger's *Malleus Maleficarum* (Hammer of Witches), published in Cologne in 1484 as a textbook of procedure against witchcraft, is particularly horrible.

Opposite: Garuda, the sacred eagle, in one of his godly guises
Below: A Brahma from South India, four-faced, and holding
sacred objects in two of his four hands

GODS

Gods have been included in this *Who's Who* for a variety of reasons: either for general interest, or because of their whole-hearted devotion to one interest – good, or evil, or love – if not simply on account of their importance.

In many mythologies there are confusions about the relationships of the gods, their marriages and affairs and children, to which inconsistencies may be attributed.

In square brackets at the end of some entries are shown correspondencies scholars have noted between the gods of different cultures, and which may indicate when a god has 'travelled' from one mythology to another. Other similarities, more general, are shown at the end of the section. Cross-references are indicated by small capital letters.

ABBREVIATIONS

A	Assyro-Babylonian	J	Japanese
AI	American Indian	M	Mexican
BA	Black African	O	Oceanic
C	Celtic	P	Phoenician
CS	Chinese	PN	Persian
E	Egyptian	PU	Peruvian
F	Finno-Ugric	R	Roman
G	Greek	S	Slavonic
H	Hindu	SA	South American
I	Indian	T	Teutonic
IR	Iranian	Y	Yucatan
IN	Incan		

ADAD A   god of the storm, but also of spring rain; able to foresee the future.

ADONIS P   beautiful agricultural god, called Tammus in the Bible. He spent half of each year on earth and half in the underworld. An eager hunter, he was killed by a wild boar. Loved by APHRODITE.

AHRIMAN PN   supreme god of darkness and the underworld, who confidently expected to triumph over the Good. A noble, if despicable, god.

AIZEN-MYOO J   god of love; fearful and ferocious, but patron of idealized platonic passion.

ALEYIN P   agricultural god of rivers, son of BA'AL; vanquished EL's son MOR in single combat.

175

Hathor, sometimes visualised as a cow, but here in beautiful human form, with her symbolic horns. Carving at Abu Simbel

AMATERASU J   sun-goddess. Frightened by the exploits of her brother SUSANOO, withdrew from the world for a while, plunging it into darkness; but was wooed back with the help of a mirror.

AMON E   King of the Gods, born from the mouth of THOTH at Thebes; sometimes seen with a ram's head. Patron of the Pharaohs, known as Amon-Ra or Aten as his power grew or diminished. Married MUT; father of KHONS.   [*Zeus*]

ANHUR E   warrior-god and great hunter; married Mehut, a lion-headed goddess.   [*Ares*]

ANUBIS E   jackal-headed guardian of the underworld and inventor of funeral-rites; son of OSIRIS and NEPTHYS.   [*Hermes*]

APHRODITE G   goddess of love and fertility, daughter of ZEUS and Dione, *or* posthumous daughter of Cronus, springing from the sea into which his castrated genitals had been cast. The most beautiful of all goddesses, awarded the apple by Paris. Possessor of an infallible aphrodisiac girdle. Married HEPHAESTUS; but innumerable lovers. [*Hathor, Isis, Venus*]

APIS E   sacred bull of PTAH; able to foretell the future.

APOLLO G   handsome sun-god, hunter (the celestial archer) and healer; god of prophecy, also a shepherd-god and a musician. Of uncertain origin, but possibly son of ZEUS and Leto; twin-brother of ARTEMIS; raised in secret because of HERA's jealousy. Founder of Delphi; a great but fatal lover. [*Horus, Mont, Shamash*]

ARES G   god of war, son of ZEUS and HERA; generally disliked, and usually defeated in battle. Had many children by various mistresses, most of whom met tragic ends.

ARTEMIS G   moon-goddess of agriculture and childbirth; daughter either of ZEUS and DEMETER or PERSEPHONE, or of DIONYSUS and ISIS, or of Leto, twin-sister of APOLLO. A great hunter and a professional virgin, fond of music and dancing.   [*Bast, Diana*]

ASSHUR A   warrior-god who supported troops in battle; also god of fertility. Married Ninlil.

Apis, the sacred bull of Ptah, the white triangle on his forehead one of the marks by which he could be recognised

Below, left: A romantic view of Freja, first of the Valkyries and their supreme commander – here shown by the nineteenth-century painter Blommer attended by cupids and in a chariot drawn by two cats!

Below, right: Anhur, 'the sky-bearer', who symbolised the creative heat of the sun. On his forehead he carried a sacred eye given to him by Ra

179

Below: Bes, the jester, in happy mood

Opposite: An Egyptian woman praying to the lovable hippopotamus-goddess Tauret, god of childbirth
Overleaf: An Allegorical Scene by Piero di Cosimo (*c* 1462–1521?). In a strange landscape, a Pan-figure mourns over the body of a maiden, wounded in the neck and wrists – perhaps by the docile dog sitting close by? The picture is poised perfectly between reality and the world of myth.

ATHENE G   goddess of war and storms, patron of the arts, protectress of heroes; daughter of ZEUS and Metis; fought valiantly in ZEUS' army; a determined virgin.   [*Sarasvati*]

AUGUST PERSONAGE OF JADE CS   Father of the Gods and creator of man.

AYA   The wife of SHAMASH; venerated with him.

BA'AL P   the symbolic name of an unnamed god, enemy of EL; son of Asherat, whom he married.

BALDER T   sun-god, son of ODIN and FRIGG. So handsome that he radiated light, he was killed in an 'accident' arranged by LOKI, and the whole world mourned for him.

BAST E   lioness- or cat-goddess, patron of musicians and dancers, with magnificent and ambitious festivals. Married PTAH.   [*Artemis*]

BES E   ugly dwarf-god of childbirth; a jester, protector against vicious animals, and an expert in toiletries.

BOCHICA SA   Colombian sun-god, Father of the Gods and inventor of all the arts.

BOR T   son of BURI, married Bestla, daughter of YMIR, and fathered the three gods ODIN, Vili and Ve, murderers of YMIR; they were all drowned in his blood.

BOREAS G   god of the north wind and companion of ZEPHYRUS, the west wind, but less rough than him.

BRAHMA I   Father of Gods and men, four-faced and four-armed; married SARASVATI, whom he created.

BRAN C   'the Blessed', a god-giant, warrior, harpist and poet, brother of Lyr; a god of fertility and patron of craftsmen.

BURI T   born of ice licked into shape by an immortal cow; father of BOR.

BUTO E   snake-goddess and nurse of HORUS.

BYELOBOG S   the white god, of light and the sun; an old man with a white beard, dressed in white, and only seen by day.

CHALCHIUHTLICUE M   goddess of marriage, babies, and chaste love. Married TLALOC, her brother.

CH'ANG-O CS   moon-goddess, who drank a cup of immortality intended for her husband, who chased her to the moon.

CHERNOBOG S   the black god of dark and evil.

CHIBCHACUM SA   god of evil who was defeated by the Colombian god BOCHICA.

CHIH-NII CS   goddess of the star Alpha, the Heavenly Spinster and daughter of the AUGUST PERSONAGE OF JADE.

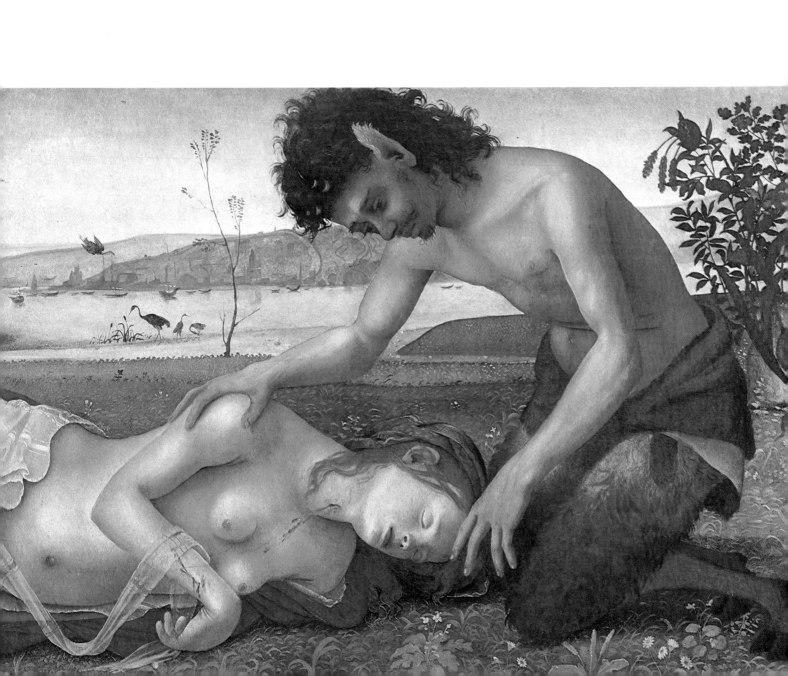

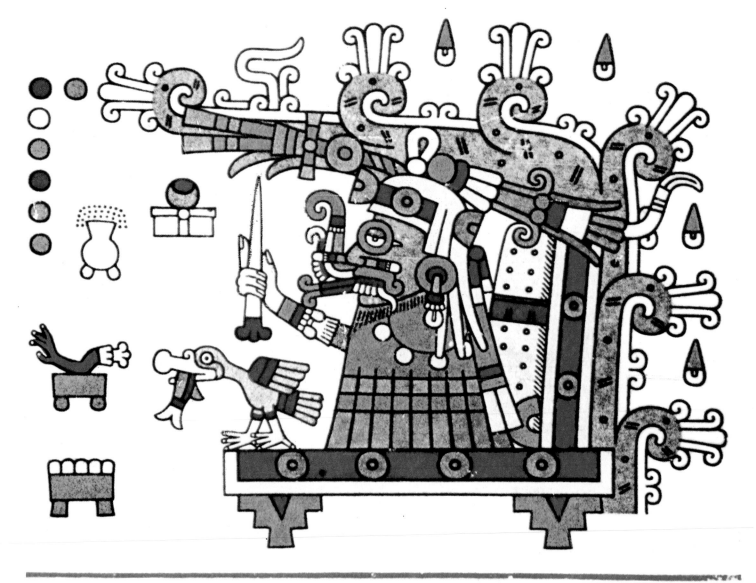

The cordial, elephant-headed Ganesa and a friendly Indian
maiden
Opposite: Tlaloc, Mexican rain-god, in his mountain-top house
of gods; his ready knife recalls the dreadful child-sacrifices
constantly made to him

Classical Minerva, goddess of handicrafts, knowledge and the arts. This is a Roman statue, but the Romans had no clear vision of her – the Etruscans showed her with wings, holding a screech-owl (sacred to Athene)

CRONUS G   son of URANUS and GAEA, who presided over the creation of the Greek pantheon. Defeated by his son ZEUS, and chained for ever between earth and sea.   [*Geb*]

CYBELE G   Phrygian goddess of caves, eventually merged with RHEA. Married Gordius, King of Phrygia.

DAGDA, The C   supreme Father of the Gods; a strong, energetic peasant-god, but also an excellent harpist.   [*Gwydion, Lug*]

DANU C   mother-goddess and daughter of the DAGDA.

DAZHBOG S   god of the sun who daily drove his gold chariot across the sky. Served by two lovely virgins, the Auroras, he ruled over the twelve kingdoms of the zodiac. Married MYESYATS, the Moon (though sometimes the latter is masculine, and Dazhbog feminine). Father of the stars.

DEMETER G   earth-goddess, daughter of CRONUS and RHEA. Raped by POSEIDON, became mother of the horse Arion; raped by ZEUS, gave birth to Kore.   [*Isis*]

DENNITSA S   one of the two Aurora sisters who tended DAZHBOG. Married the Moon; mother of the stars.

DIANA R   the Roman counterpart of ARTEMIS, the chaste hunter.

DIONYSUS G   god of wine, son of ZEUS and Semele (daughter of the King of Thebes). Discovered the art of wine-making, and travelled the world teaching it to man, attended by satyrs, Sileni, Pans, Priapi, centaurs and nymphs, and by his libidinous tutor Silenus. Charming as a youth, became god of extremity and excess, especially sexual. Married Ariadne, Minos' daughter.   [*Osiris*]

DIS PATER R   god of death and richest of all the gods.

DONAR   see THOR.

EA A   or Enki to the Sumerians, was god of knowledge and patron of workers; he guarded the waters on which the earth floated. Married Ninki; father of MARDUK.   [*Poseidon*]

EL P   god of Canaan, who existed before any other Phoenician gods.

EMMA-HOO J   god of Jigoku, the Japanese Buddhist hell, who judged men, reflecting all their sins back into their eyes through a gigantic mirror.

ENKI   see EA.

ENLIL A   Sumerian god of the air, who was assimilated into the Babylonian god MARDUK or BEL; he then became King of the Earth, and weighed good against evil. He married Ninlil, Ninkhursag or Belit.   [*Zeus*]

EOS G   goddess of dawn. Married Astraeus, by whom she bore the winds; also married Tithonus, for whom she begged the gift of immortality without thinking also to request immortal youth. He became the oldest old man in Olympus.

EROS G   youngest and most mischievous of the gods; son of APHRODITE and ARES, HERMES or ZEUS (though perhaps of Ilithyia or IRIS). An arrow from his bow shot love into the heart of whomever it hit.   [*Cupid*]

FAUNUS R   lawgiver and god of fertility; grandson of SATURN.

FREY T   son of NJÖRD and Skadi; he married Gerda, a giant's daughter, and had many adventures, succumbing in battle, finally, after losing his magic sword.

FREYJA T   the leading Valkyrie; extremely beautiful. Not to be confused with FRIGG or Frija. A twin-sister of FREY, she received dead heroes in her banqueting-hall in the sky; not notably chaste.

FRIGG T   or Frija; protectress of marriage and bringer of children. Wife of ODIN, who did not always receive support from her.

FRIJA   see FRIGG.

GAEA G   goddess of earth, mother of URANUS and creator of the universe; patroness of marriage.

GANESA I   fat, elephant-headed and amiable god of riches and success; patron of literature.

GA-OH AI   the giant who commanded the winds.

GAYOMART Pn   creator of the first human beings.

GEB E   Father of the Gods and third divine Pharoah. Successor to SHU. Married his sister NUT; father of OSIRIS and SET.

GWYDION C   all-powerful British father-god; magician and poet.

HADES G   god of the underworld; son of CRONUS and RHEA. Married PERSEPHONE, DEMETER's daughter, whom he abducted.   [*Osiris, Pluto*]

HAPI E   god of the Nile, with a woman's breasts.

HATHOR E   daughter of RA, sky-goddess and the great cow which gave birth to the world. Patroness of music and the dance, fond of alcohol. Married HORUS. See also SEKHMET.   [*Aphrodite*]

HEBE G   goddess of youth, herself eternally young. Daughter of ZEUS and HERA. Married Hercules.

HECATE G   moon-goddess, patron of rich men, sailors and flocks. Daughter of ZEUS and HERA, and disowned by the latter for stealing her cosmetics; became guardian of the underworld.

HEIMDALL T   sun-god who guarded Bifröst, the rainbow bridge to the world of the gods; great enemy of LOKI.   [*Janus*]

HEL T   goddess-guardian of the underworld, possibly a daughter of LOKI, brought up with the terrible wolf Fenrir and the great serpent Midgard. Half of her face was human, the other half a blank.

HELIOS G   the Sun himself, who drives his golden chariot daily across the sky. All-seeing god of light. Married Perse, Neaera, Rhode, GAEA, Iphinoë and Clymene – by whom he fathered Phaethon. [*Shamash*]

HEPHAESTUS G   immortal crippled blacksmith of Olympus, son of ZEUS and HERA. God of fire. Married APHRODITE (by blackmail, having kidnapped her mother); many children by other liaisons.   [*Ptah*]

188   *HERA* G   virgin queen of the sky, eldest daughter

of CRONUS and RHEA, who married ZEUS and became patron of all womanly activities. Sometimes jealous of her husband's infidelities, and not infrequently vindictive (as when, Paris preferring APHRODITE's beauty to her own, she arranged the complete annihilation of the Trojan race). [*Isis, Nut*]

HERMES G god of travellers and messenger of ZEUS (his father, by Maia). Escorted the souls of the dead to the underworld. A great athlete and lover of goddesses and women; father of PAN. [*Anubis*]

HESTIA G goddess of the domestic hearth; eldest daughter of CRONUS and RHEA, and the oldest of the Olympic gods. Both POSEIDON and APOLLO proposed to her, but she remained a virgin.

HIRUKU J god of the early morning son; grandson of AMATERASU.

HORUS E sun-god; posthumous son of OSIRIS, recognized as his true heir after much litigation against SET, his uncle. Over twenty individual Horuses were identified, among the variations being Haroeris, Behdety, Harakhtes and Hariensis. [*Apollo*]

HUITZILOPOCHTLI M god of war, son of the good Coatlicue, his conception signalled to her by a wreath of feathers falling from the sky. Protector of the Aztecs.

HUNAB KU Y King of the Gods, god of the sun, inventor of weaving. Married Ixazaluoh, goddess of water.

INDRA I all-powerful warrior-god who rides in his chariot the sun; victor over the great dragon Vritra. God, too, of nature. [*Zeus*]

INTI In sun-god whose face was set in flame; only the Incas, descended from him, were permitted to pronounce his name.

IRIS G general servant to the gods; ZEUS' private messenger and personal body-servant of HERA.

ISHTAR A personification of the planet Venus; daughter of Anu or SIN, and goddess of love or war. Ill-tempered and unreliable.

ISIS E eldest daughter of GEB and NUT; instituted

the ceremony of marriage; recovered the dismembered body of her husband and elder brother, OSIRIS, and invented embalming before resurrecting him. The mother of HORUS. [*Demeter, Hera, Selene, Aphrodite*]

ITZAMNA Y   god of resurrection and great healer; inventor of the visual arts and of writing.

IZANAGI and *IZANAMI* J   brother and sister creators of the countries of the world, and of many gods.

JANUS R   the one truly Roman god, sun-god of gates and entrances.

JUMALA F   sky-god and Father of the Gods.

JUNO R   moon-goddess of childbirth and fertility. Married to JUPITER, her brother.

JUPITER R   god of the sun and moon and storms; later patron of Rome and her empire. Married his sister JUNO.

KAGU-ZUCHI J   the fire-god, especially protective of geishas.

KHNUM E   goat-god of procreation, sculptor of mankind who shaped children in the womb. Married to both Sati and Anukis.

KHONS E   a moon-god, bald except for a single lock of hair. Adopted by AMON and MUT, he became a popular healer. [*Hercules*]

KITCKI MANITOU AI   all-powerful spirit of the Algonquin Indians, god of the sun and winds.

KRISHNA I   an incarnation of VISHNU; a charming, handsome, amorous, bold and upright immortal hero.

K'UEI-HSLING CS   extremely ugly god of examinations, who selects successful candidates.

LOGE T   see LOKI.

LOKI T   a highly mischievous, almost demonaic god of fire, blood-brother of ODIN. A handsome and loquacious seducer and inveterate plotter against his fellow-gods, who foretold *Götterdämmerung*, or the end of the gods' world. [*Lug*]

Agnolo Bronzino (1503–72), a Florentine portraitist, painted Andrea Doria, a famous naval captain, in the apt complimentary role of Neptune

LUG c   a sun-god, master of many skills; a warrior armed with a sling.   [*Gwydion, Dagda, Loki*]

LUONNOTAR f   creator of the world, hatching it from a duck's egg as she floated in primeval waters.

MACHA c   Irish fertility and mother-goddess; a warrior who built the fortress Emain Macha. She died there giving birth to twins after racing against the horses of Conchobor.

MAMA QUILLA In   moon-goddess, sister and wife of the Sun, INTI; patroness of married women.

MANANNÁN c   god of the sea beneath which he lived in Tir na nOc, the underworld.

MARDUK A   son of EA, and god of agriculture, who fought the dreadful Tiamat. He rationalized the universe, fixing the planets' courses, and created man.

MARS R   agricultural god, later god of war; son of JUNO. Married Rhea Silvia to become father of Romulus, founder of Rome.   [*Tyr*]

MATI-SYRA-ZEMLYA s   goddess earth, who could predict the future and was infallibly just.

MAZDA Pn   god of the Persian kings and creator of all things, abstract and infallible.

MERCURY R   god of commerce.

MICHABO AI   the Algonquin Indian Big Rabbit, creator of mankind.

MIN E   ancient god of fertility, travellers and agriculture.   [*Pan*]

MINEPA BA   Zambesi god of all evil.

MINERVA R   goddess of education and business; later, a war-goddess.   [*Athene*]

MITHRA Ir   the great warrior-god, associated too with the sun and with light; bringer of victory and of wisdom, guardian against lying and cheating. [*Mars, Mitra, Tyr*]

MITRA I   god of the day, friendship and legal agreements.   [*Mars, Mithra, Tyr*]

MONT E   sun-god of war, sometimes with the head of a bull. Married Rat-tau.   [*Apollo*]

MOT P   god of the harvest, son of EL; vanquished by ALEYIN, son of BA'AL.

MUT E   sky-goddess in the form of a cow, sometimes confused with BAST or SEKHMET. Married Amon-Ra (see AMON); adoptive mother of MONT and KHONS.   [*Hera*]

MYESYATS s   the Moon. Married the Sun (or DEMETER or Aurora) and mother (or father, for sometimes she is masculine) of the stars.

MY LORD THUNDER J   extremely ugly god of the elements; punishes great criminals.

NDRIANANAHARY BA   supreme god of the Negroes of Madagascar, dispenser of life-giving rain.

NEITH E   one of the oldest Egyptian gods: a warrior but also a weaver, said to be the mother of RA. A celestial cow, she gave birth to the sky, and wove the earth from nothing. [*Pallas Athene*]

NEKHEBET E   patroness of childbirth.

NEPTHYS E   daughter of GEB and NUT, she watched over the bodies of the dead; she married her brother SET, but seduced her other brother OSIRIS and bore his son ANUBIS.

NEREUS G   'Old Man of the Sea', able to foretell the future. Son of Pontus and GAEA, he married Doris and fathered the Nereids – over fifty of them.

'NG AI BA   the Masai god and creator of the universe.

NINURTH A   god of war and hunting, son of ENLIL; married Bau, daughter of ANU.

NIPARAYA AI   creator of the universe, named by the Perico Indians; married Amayicoyondi.

NJÖRD T   an agricultural god, one of the Vanir, who seems to have been bisexual but married Skadi, a giant's daughter, who selected him in mistake for BALDER. Father of FREY.

Sarasvati, wife of Brahma, who created her. He was so overcome by her beauty that he grew three extra heads expressly to be able to watch her. A carving from Orissa in East India

NOKOMIS AI   the earth-mother, named by the Algonquin Indians.

NUADA C   a hero-god with one silver hand and a sword so powerful that it could not be resisted.

NUN E   Father of the Gods; spent his life up to his waist in the primeval ocean.

NUT E   sky-goddess, who sometimes takes the shape of a cow, the stars shining on her belly. She married her twin brother GEB, against RA's wishes; the mother of OSIRIS, SET, ISIS and NEPTHYS. [*Rhea*]

OCEANUS G   the powerful god of the waters, son of URANUS and GAEA; married his sister Tethys, and became father of three thousand rivers.

ODIN or *WODIN* T   handsome, eloquent god of the human spirit and patron of heroes; a poet who made all human laws. A great warrior who held court at Valhalla, he fatally wounded himself in order to be reborn as a youth. Married FRIGG or FREYA.   [*Mercury*]

OLD-SPIDER O   According to Nauru islanders, creator of the universe.

ORMAZD Pn   supreme god of light, creator of the universe, commander of the six great immortals of Persian myth.

OSIRIS E   god of the dead, elder son of GEB and NUT, he built the earliest temples and civilized the known world. Murdered by his brother SET, he was restored to life by his wife ISIS. Father (posthumously) of HORUS.   [*Dionysus, Hades*]

O-WATA-TSU-MI or *SHIO-ZUCHI* J   patron of all sea-creatures and sailors.

PACHACAMAC P   Father of the Gods; a fire-god, made by the Incas god of the sun; so great that he could not be represented in any visible form.

PAN G   son of HERMES, by a doubtful mother – perhaps Dryope, or the nymph Oeneis, or Odysseus' wife Penelope, or Amaltheia the goat. So ugly at birth that his mother rejected him, and he became a sort of court jester to the gods. Guardian of flocks and herds, a determined seducer (he claimed to have seduced all the maenads).   [*Min*]

Vishnu in one of his *avatars*, or descents into life, tears the belly
from a dying demon. A bronze at Hanuman Dhoka, Katmandu,
Nepal

Quetzalcoatl, snake-bird, god of wind, master of life, patron of arts, a bearded man here wearing his usual mask of a short-snouted animal. A seventh – eighth-century shell mosaic from Tula, Mexico

PERSEPHONE G   goddess of the underworld, daughter of ZEUS and DEMETER, abducted by HADES, who married her.

PLUTO R   Roman counterpart of HADES.

POSEIDON G   god of the sea, once the equal of his brother ZEUS. Son of CRONUS and RHEA, given domination over the oceans. Married Amphitrite, daughter of OCEANUS, he had many liaisons and numberless children.   [*Ea*]

PROTEUS G   'Old Man of the Sea', and guardian of seals.

PTAH E   a mummy-god, patron of artists and workmen, only less important than AMON and RA in the Egyptian pantheon. Protector against evil. Married SEKHMET and BAST.   [*Hephaestus*]

QUETZALCOATL M   god of wind, driven from Mexico by TEZCATLIPOCA.

RA E   the great sun-god, creator and king of the world; all living things were born of his tears. Possibly the son of NEITH.

RHEA G   Mother of the Gods, eventually merged with CYBELE. Married CRONUS. [*Nut*]

RUDRA I   prince of evil and creator of SIVA.

SARASVATI I   goddess of music, wisdom and knowledge; inventor of Sanskrit. Created by, then wife of, BRAHMA.   [*Athene*]

SATURN R   agricultural god of vineyards and fields. Once King of Italy, driven from the sky by JUPITER; founder of the Saturnalia.

SAVITRI I   god of all moving things, king of heaven and god of immortality.

SEBEK E   crocodile-god who aided SET in the murder of OSIRIS.

SEDNA   Eskimo goddess of the sea and sea-creatures.

SEKHMET E   the goddess HATHOR, renamed when she became the violent persecutor of the evil opponents of RA. Married PTAH.

SELENE G   moon-goddess, sister of HELIOS, or perhaps his daughter; or perhaps a daughter of ZEUS, by whom she had three daughters. Among the many goddesses seduced by PAN. [*Iris*]

SESHAT E   goddess of history and mistress of the library. Married THOTH.

SET E   evil, red-haired son of GEB and NUT, and assassinator of his brother OSIRIS. Spirit of evil, sometimes represented as an ugly and vicious animal. Married his sister NEPTHYS.   [*Typhon*]

SHAMASH A   sun-god, antagonist of night and winter, who could foretell the future. Married AYA; father of Kittu (Justice) and Misaru (Law). [*Apollo, Helios*]

SHINA-TSU-HIKO J   god of wind, which fills the space between heaven and earth.

SHOU-HSING CS   god of longevity, who presides over all old folks' birthdays, and decides the dates of all deaths.

SHU E   son of RA, succeeding him as earthly king; abdicated in favour of his son GEB. Married his sister TEFNUT.

SIN A   moon-god and father of SHAMASH (the Sun) and ISHTAR (Venus). Enemy of wickedness and measurer of time. Married Ningal; father of Nusku, god of fire.

SIVA I   god of asceticism, leader of demons and evil spirits; a great dancer. Married Parvati (who had other names, including Uma and Kali).

SURYA I   sun-god, married Sanjna, who bore him three children before being overwhelmed by his brilliance.

SUSANOO J   god of the seas, son of IZANAGI, driven out of heaven for his wicked deeds.

SVAROG S   god of the sky, father of DAZHBOG (the Sun) and Svarogich (Fire).

T'AI-YUEH-TA-TI CS   organizer of the lives of all human beings.

TAWISCARA AI   an amalgum of all evil forces,   197

The wife of the god Siva took at least ten forms including Yuma, Parvati and (below) Durga. While Parvati was kind and gentle and Yuma a stern ascetic, Durga was an invincible heroin who destroyed a giant demon

much given to procreation but able only to produce monsters.

TEFNUT E   woman with the head of a lioness; goddess of rain. Married her brother SHU.

TEZCATLIPOCA M   sun-god of music and dancing. Great enemy of QUETZALCOATL; received many blood-sacrifices.

THEMIS G   goddess of justice, housekeeper to the gods and muse to ZEUS; midwife at the births of APOLLO and ARTEMIS. Married ZEUS.

THOR or *DONAR* T   god of thunder and of war, a noble but brutal and much-feared immortal armed with a stone hammer. Married Sif; father of Magni (Force) and Modi (Choler).

THOTH E   Ibis-headed son of GEB and NUT or of RA; moon-god and patron of science and literature; inventor of hieroglyphs, herald of the gods. Ruled Egypt for 3,226 years. Married Maat, Seshat and Nehmauit.   [*Hermes*]

THUNDERBIRD AI   Almost all American Indians believe the Thunderbird to be one of the most important of all immortal spirits; he keeps crops growing and waters the earth.

T'IEN HOU CS   sea-goddess and princess of supernatural favour; finally, empress of heaven, patroness of all sailors.

TIRAWA AI   ruler of the universe, as named by the Pawnee Indians.

TLALOC M   bloodthirsty god of mountains and ruins; married CHALCHIUHTLICUE, his sister.

TORNGASOAU   immortal Eskimo god who was supreme over the spirits.

TS'AI-SHEN CS   god of riches, treated with enormous respect and deference.

TSAO-WANG CS   god of domestic fire, who reports annually on the activities of men to the AUGUST PERSONAGE OF JADE.

TSUKI-YOMI J   god or goddess of the moon.

TUONETAR F   mistress of Tuonela, the underworld; married Tuoni, only less horrid than her.

TYPHON G   the largest monster ever born, child of Tartarus and Earth. From the thighs downwards, he was a mass of coiled snakes; his arms, with snakes' heads for fingers, reached a hundred leagues in each direction. Managed once to capture ZEUS, who was rescued by PAN and HERMES. Now imprisoned beneath Mount Etna.   [*Set*]

TYR T   a sky-god once thought to have been the father of all Teutonic gods.   [*Mitra, Mars*]

TZINTEOTL M   goddess of procreation and of the birth of all things.

UKKO F   successor to JUMALA as supreme god; married Akka, goddess of the mountain ash.

URANUS G   father (by his mother GAEA) of the twelve Titans, the three Cyclopes, and three monsters. Castrated by his son CRONUS; from his blood the Furies were born, and from his severed genitals, thrown into the sea, sprang APHRODITE.

USHAS I   daughter of heaven, sister of the night, goddess of the dawn, wife of the Sun and mistress of fire. She awakens all creation each morning, for the day's activities.

VARUNA I   all-seeing god of the moon and of oaths; regulates the working of the universe. [*O-Wata-Tsu-Mi*]

VENUS R   goddess of vegetable gardens, later associated with APHRODITE as goddess of love.

VESTA R   goddess of fire, who prepared the food of the gods; served, on earth, by the vestal virgins.

VIRACOCHA Pu   sun-god who lived in a lake, made the sun moon and stars, and created man.

VISHNU I   supreme god of light; married Lakshmi.

VULCAN R   sun-god of fire and creative warmth, bearing HEPHAESTUS' hammer and anvil; born of a human girl on to whom a spark fell from heaven.

WAKONDA AI   ruler of the universe, named by the Sioux Indians.

WEN CH'ANG CS   god of literature, who obtained the post after living seventeen exemplary lives.

WODIN   see ODIN.

YMIR T   the first of all living creatures, father of the giants, who were born of his sweat. The earth was later made of his body.

ZEPHYRUS G   god of the west wind, originally rough and forceful, but later tamed, perhaps by his marriage to Chloris.

ZEUS G   supreme god, judge and ruler of gods and men. Married Eurynome, Metis, Mnemosyne and others; official consort, HERA. Innumerable liaisons with goddesses and humans.   [*Amon, Enlil, Indra*]

General Correspondencies

Here are lists of some gods and goddesses of various mythological pantheons whose positions or duties correspond.

Creators of man The August Personage of Jade, Brahma, Gayomart, Khnum, Luonnotar, Marduk, Michabo, Ng-ai, Niparaya, Old-Spider, Ra, Viracocha.

Gods of agriculture Adonis, Aleyin, Artemis, Marduk, Mars, Min, Mot, Njörd, Saturn, Thunderbird.

Gods of the arts Athene, Bast, Hathor, Ptah, Sarasvati, Seshat, Thoth.

Gods of the earth Cybele, Demeter, Gaes, Mati-Syra-Zemlya, Nokomis, Rhea.

Gods of evil Ahriman, Chibchacum, Loki, Minepa, Rudra, Set, Siva, Tawiscara.

Gods of the intellect and knowledge Ea, Ganesa, Itzamna, K'uei-hsing, Minerva, Sarasvati, Wen-Ch'ang.

Gods of justice Enlil, Faunus, Mati-Syra-Zemlya.

Gods of love Aizen-Myoo, Aphrodite, Eros, Ishtar, Venus.

Gods of marriage Chalchiuhtlicue, Frigg, Gaea, Isis, Juno, Mamma Quilla.

Gods of procreation   Aphrodite, Faunus, Khnum, Tzinteotl.

Gods of the sea   Manannán, Nereus, Oceanus, O-Wata-Tsu-Mi, Proteus, T'ien Hou.

Gods of the underworld   Anubis, Dis Pater, Emma-Hoo, Hades, Hecate, Hel, Hermes, Osiris, Persephone, Pluto, Tuonetar and Tuoni.

Gods of the winds   Adad, Boreas, My Lord Thunder, Shina-Tsu-Hiko, Zephyrus.

Kings or Fathers of the Gods   Amon, The August Personage of Jade, Bochica, Brahma, the Dagda, Geb, Hunab, Indra, Jumala, Kitcki Manitou, Mazda, Nun, Pachacamac, Tirawa, Torngasoau, Ukko, Wakonda, Zeus.

Moon-gods   Artemis, Ch'ang-o, Hecate, Juno, Khons, Mama Quilla, Myesyats, Selene, Sin, Thoth, Tsuki-Yomi, Varuna.

Sun-gods   Amaterasu, Apollo, Balder, Bochica, Byelobog, Dazhbog, Heimdall, Helios, Hiruku, Horus, Inti, Janus, Jupiter, Lug, Ra, Shamash, Surya, Tezcatlipoca, Viracocha, Vishnu, Vulcan.

Warrior-gods   Anhur, Ares, Asshur, Athene, Huitzilopochtli, Ishtar, Lug, Macha, Mars, Minerva, Mont, Neith, Ninurta, Sekhmet.

The Mirror of Myths

Many of the immortal figures of myth have much the same personality whether they appear in the mythology of Greece or China, Japan or Oceania or the Teutons – just as the legendary accounts of creation, of the punishments reserved for wrongdoers, or of the obtaining of fire or the invention of death, bear much resemblance each to each. Here are a few of the more obvious correspondencies:

The arts
The arts – which encompass usefulness (i.e. the invention of pottery) – were often taught to man by a particular god: Bacchus, Cadmus (the Greeks), Cagn (South African bushmen), Manco Capac (Peruvians), Michabo (the Algonquin Indians), Nuada of the Silver Hand (Celts), Oannes (Babylonia), Okikurimi (Japanese), Osiris (Egyptians), Prometheus (Greeks), Pund-jel (Australians), Quetzalcoatl (Mexicans), Wieland the Smith (Scandinavians).

Death
Death is the great Unnatural, and to account for it many varied legends grew up. Usually, there was some original sin which resulted in man being cursed with this terrible evil.

AUSTRALIANS   woman approached a forbidden tree too closely.

CENTRAL AFRICANS   at first, sleep was unknown; a woman offered to teach man how to sleep, but held his nose too long. He died.

FIJI ISLANDERS   a rat opposed the Moon's plan that man should be regularly reborn like herself. The rat won, and men die like rats.

GREEKS   death came as a result of lifting the lid of Pandora's box.

HINDUS   Yama led man to the Other World.

HURONS   the living were destroyed by the moon.

NEW ZEALANDERS (Maoris)   Mani was not properly baptized.

PENTECOST ISLANDERS   Tagar made men die for five days only and live again; but Suque opposed this, and victory was his.

SOUTHERN INDIA   death bit man while God slept.

Dismemberment
In the mythology of several cultures, a god was torn to pieces and the pieces scattered and afterwards recovered. Osiris and Isis are the characters of the story in Egypt; in Greece, Dionysus and Demeter. The bushmen speak of the moon being cut to pieces by the sun, and the Finns, Romanians, Russians, Indians of Brazil and natives of Madagascar and Polynesia have similar stories.

Fire-stealing

The incalculably valuable element, fire, was stolen from God, or the gods, in a number of myths. Among the thieves were the Coyote (Cahrocs and Navaho Indians), the Golden-coated Wren (Bretons), a man who became a bird (the Murri tribe of Gippsland, Australia), Mani (New Zealanders), Matarisvan (Vedas), Prometheus (Greeks), Quawteaht (Ahts Indians), and Teyn the Raven (Athapascan Indians).

Good versus Evil

ALGONQUIN INDIANS   Michabo *v.* the Prince of Serpents

AUSTRALIANS   Pund-jel (the Eagle) *v.* the Crow (Evil)

BABYLONIANS   Marduk *v.* Tiamat

EGYPTIANS   Osiris *v.* Set

GREEKS   Zeus *v.* Typhon; Apollo *v.* Python

HOTTENTOTS   Caunab (Evil) *v.* Tsui-Goab (Good)

HURON INDIANS   Joskeha *v.* Tawiscara

INDIANS   Indra *v.* Vitra

INCAS   Piguerao (Day) *v.* Apocatequil (Night)

PERSIANS   Ormazd *v.* Ahriman

TEUTONS   Thor *v.* Loki

The moon

The moon is personalized in most myths:

ALGONQUINS   the same word means moon, night, death, cold, sleep and water.

BABYLONIANS   Sin is the moon-goddess.

BRAZILIAN INDIANS   mothers shelter their children from the harmful rays of the moon.

EGYPTIANS   Isis inflicts illnesses on the cursed.

GREEKS   Selene is moon-goddess.

ROMANS   Diana or Luna rules the moon.

A place of punishment

Most myths have this in common:

BABYLONIANS   Allatu presides over Sheol or Aralu.

CELTS   Annwn is unruled, but ever-present.

EGYPTIANS   Osiris presides over Amenti.

GREEKS   Pluto and Persephone preside over Hades or Tartarus.

GUATEMALANS   HunCame presides over Xibalba.

JAPAN   Emma-Hoo presides over Jigoku.

MEXICANS   Mictlantecutli presides over Mictlan.

Selective Reading List

An enormous number of books on myth in general, and the mythology of various races in particular, have been published during the past century. Only a few published before 1900 have been included in this list, which suggests further reading. The date following each title is that of first publication in the English language.

Allen, Don C, *Mysteriously Meant* (1970)
Anesaki, Mahasaru, *History of Japanese Religion* (1930)
Archer, WG, *The Loves of Krishna* (1957)
Armstrong, John HS, *The Paradise Myth* (1969)
Aston, WG, *Nihongi: Chronicles of Japan* (1956)
Astour, Michael C, *Hellenosemitica* (1965)

Bailey, James RS, *The God-Kings and the Titans* (1973)
Barthes, R, *Mythologies* (1957)
Beckwith, M, *Hawaiian Mythology* (1940)
Bellamy, HS, *Moons, Myths &c.* (1949)
Bennett, AG, *Focus on the Unknown* (1953)
Borges, Jorge L, and Guerrero, M, *The Book of Imaginary Beings* (1970)
Brandon, SGF, *Creation Legends of the Ancient Near East* (1963)
Branston, B, *The Lost Gods of England* (1957)
Brophy, Brigid, *Black Ship to Hell* (1962)
Bulfinch, T, *The Golden Age of Myth and Legend* (1926)
——, *The Age of Fable* (1927)
Burland, Cottie, *The Gods of Mexico* (1967)
Butler, EM, *Myth of the Magus* (1949)
Butterworth, Edric AS, *The Tree at the Navel of the World* (1970)

Caillois, R, *The Mask of Medusa* (1964)
Campbell, Joseph, *The Masks of God* (1965)
——, *The Hero with a Thousand Faces* (1968)
Cardinall, AW, *Tales Told in Togoland* (1931)
Carpenter, R, *Folk Tales, Fiction and Saga in Homeric Epics* (1946)
Cassirer, E, *Language and Myth* (1955)

Cerny, J, *Ancient Egyptian Religions* (1952)
Chadwick, HM, *The Heroic Age* (1912)
Chaplin, D, *Matter, Myth and Spirit* (1935)
Clark, Anne, *Beasts and Bawdy* (1975)
Cles-Reden, SE von, *The Realm of the Great Goddess* (1961)
Cook, AB, *Zeus* (1914–25)
Cook, Elizabeth, *The Ordinary and the Fabulous* (1969)
Cook, Roger, *The Tree of Life* (1974)
Cooke, HP, *Osiris* (1931)
Courtney, RA, *The Hill and the Circle* (1912)
Cox, GW, *An Introduction to the Science of Comparative Myth and Folklore* (1881)
Crawford, OGS, *The Eye Goddess* (1957)

Daniel, GE, and Page, DL, *Myth or Legend* (1955)
Dawson, C, *The Age of the Gods* (1928)
Dorson, Richard M., *Peasant Customs and Savage Myths* (1968)
Drioton, Etienne, *The Religion of the Ancient East* (1959)
Driver, GR, *Canaanite Myths and Legends* (1956)
Downing, C, *Russian Tales and Legends* (1956)
Duffy, Maureen, *The Erotic World of Faery* (1970)
Dunne, John S, *The City of the Gods* (1974)

Elderkin, GW, *Kantharos: Dionysus* (1924)
Eliade, Mircea, *Myths, Dreams and Mysteries* (1960)
——, *The Sacred and the Profane* (1961)
——, *Myth and Reality* (1964)
——, *The Two and the One* (1965)
——, *From Primitive to Zen* (1967)
Ellis, HR Davidson, *Gods and Myths of Northern Europe* (1964)

Frankfurt, H, *Kingship and the Gods* (1948)
Frazer, Sir James G, *The Golden Bough* (1890–1915; various editions)
——, *Belief in Immortality and the Worship of the Dead* (1927)
——, *Myths of the Origin of Fire* (1930)
Freden, G, *Orpheus and the Goddess of Nature* (1958)
Freund, PH, *Mysteries of Creation* (1964)
Fromm, E, *Forgotten Language* (1952)

Gadd, CJ, *Ideas of Divine Rule in the Ancient East* (1948)
Gardner, P, *Origins of Myth* (1896)

Gaster, Theodor H, *Thespis* (1950)
——, *Myth, Custom and Legend in the Old Testament* (1961)
Gayley, CM, *Classical Myths in English Literature* (1911)
Genner, A van, *Rites of Passage* (1960)
Gimbutas, Marija B, *The Gods and Goddesses of Old Europe* (1974)
Gordon, CH, *Before the Bible* (1962)
Grant, Michael, *Myths of the Greeks and Romans* (1962)
Graves, Robert, *The White Goddess* (1948)
——, *The Greek Myths* (1955)
Gray, John, *Near Eastern Mythology* (1969)
Grey, Sir George, *Polynesian Mythology* (1855; new edition 1956)
Griffiths, John G, *The Conflict of Horus and Seth* (1960)
Guthrie, WKC, *Myth and Reason* (1953)

Harden, DE, *The Phoenicians* (1962)
Harris, JR, *The Cult of the Heavenly Twins* (1906)
——, *Picus Who Is Also Zeus* (1916)
Hartland, ES, *Ritual and Belief* (1914)
Hatt, G, *Asiatic Influence in American Folklore* (1949)
Henderson, JL, *Ancient Myths and Modern Man* (1964)
Henning, WB, *Zoroaster* (1951)
Hinks, RP, *Myth and Allegory in Ancient Art* (1939)
Hocart, AM, *Life-Giving Myth* (1952)
Hooke, SH (ed.), *Myth and Ritual* (1933)
——, *The Labyrinth* (1935)
——, *The Siege Perilous* (1953)
—— (ed.), *Myth, Ritual and Kingship* (1958)
——, *Middle Eastern Myth* (1963)
Howells, WW, *The Heathens* (1949)
Hungerford, EB, *Slaves of Darkness* (1941)
Huxley, Francis, *The Way of the Sacred* (1974)

Ions, Veronica, *Indian Mythology* (1967)

James, EO, *The Nature and Function of Priesthood* (1956)
——, *Prehistoric Religions* (1957)
——, *Myth and Ritual in the Ancient Near East* (1958)
——, *The Cult of the Mother-Goddess* (1959)
——, *The Ancient Gods* (1960)
Jayne, WA, *Healing Gods of Ancient Civilisations* (1925)
Jung, CG, and Kerényi, *Essays on a Science of Myth* (1949)

Kavanagh, Morgan P, *The Origin of Language and Myth* (1871)

Kellett, EE, *The Story of Myths* (1928)

Kirk, Geoffrey S, *Myth, Its Meaning and Function in Ancient and Other Cultures* (1971)

Kuhn, AB, *The Lost Light* (1948)

Lang, A, *Custom and Myth* (1910)

Leach, Sir Edmund (ed.), *The Structural Study of Myth and Totemism* (1964)

Leglay, Marcel, *Saturne Africain* (1966)

Lethbridge, Thomas C, *Gogmagog* (1957)

Levi-Strauss, Claude, *The Raw and the Cooked* (1970)

Lindberger, Ö, *Transformations of Amphitryon* (1956)

Lissner, I, *Man, God and Magic* (1961)

Lump, P, *Stars in Our Heaven* (1951)

McConnel, Ursula, *Myths of the Muncan* (1957)

MacCulloch, JA, *Medieval Faith and Fable* (1932)

Malinowski, B, *Myth in Primitive Psychology* (1932)

——, *Magic, Science and Religion* (1949)

——, *Sex Cultures and Myth* (1963)

Manuel, FE, *The Eighteenth Century Confronts the Gods* (1959)

Maringer, J, *Gods of Prehistoric Man* (1960)

Mason, JA, *The Ancient Civilisations of Peru* (1957)

Murray, AS, *Manual* (1936)

Murray, MA, *Ancient Egyptian Legends* (1913)

Neumann, E, *Origins and History of Consciousness* (1954)

——, *The Great Mother* (1955)

Olcott, WT, *Star Lore of All Ages* (1911)

Onians, RB, *The Origins of European Thought* (1954)

Paracelsus, AT, *A Book of Nymphs, Sylphs &c.* (1941)

Parrinder, EG, *African Mythology* (1968)

Patch, Howard R, *The Other World According to the Descriptions of Medieval Literature* (1970)

Pettazzoni, R, *The All-Knowing God* (1956)

Plongéon, A Le, *Sacred Mysteries Among the Mayas* (1909)

Plutarch, *Isis and Osiris* (various editions)

Poignant, Roslyn, *Oceanic Mythology* (1968)

Porteous, A, *Forest Folklore* (1928)

Raglan, FRS, *The Hero* (1936)

Reik, T, *Myth and Guilt* (1958)

Righter, William H, *Myth and Literature* (1975)

Rogers, JET, *Bible Folklore* (1884)

Rotheim, Geza, *The Panic of the Gods* (1972)

Seznec, Jean J, *The Survival of the Pagan Gods* (1972)

Sjoestedt, Marie Louise, *Gods and Heroes of the Celts* (1967)

Smart, Roderic N, *The Phenomenon* (1968)

Smith, EW, and Parrinder, EG, *African Ideas of God* (1967)

Smith, GE, *Evolution of the Dragon* (1919)

Spence, L, *Myth and Ritual in Dance, Games, &c.* (1947)

Spevack-Husmann, H, *The Mighty Pan* (1963)

Thomas, K, *Religion and the Decline of Magic* (1971)

Thompson, RL, *History of the Devil* (1929)

Tooke, A, *Pantheon: The Fabulous History of the Heathen Gods* (1729)

Vaillant, GC, *The Aztecs of Mexico* (1952)

Vermaseren, MJ, *Mithras, the Secret God* (1963)

Ward, JSM, *Freemasonry and the Ancient Gods* (1921)

Warner, Rex, *Men and Gods* (1952)

Werner, ETC, *Myths and Legends of China* (1922)

Zimmer, H, *The King and the Corpse* (1948)

Encyclopedias and Dictionaries

Bernen, Satia, and Bernen, R, *Myth and Religion in European Painting, 1270–1700* (1973)

Dowson, J, *Classical Dictionary of Hindu Mythology* (1961)

Funk & Wagnalls Standard Dictionary of Folklore (1949–50)

Grant, Michael, and Hazel, J, *Who's Who in Classical Mythology* (1973)

Larousse Encyclopaedia of Mythology (1959)

MacCulloch, John A, and Gray, Louis H, *The Mythology of All Races* (1922)

Robinson, HS, and Wilson, K, *Encyclopaedia of Myths and Legends of All Nations* (1962)

Sykes, E, *Everyman's Dictionary of Non-Classical Mythology* (1952)

Quick Reference

In alphabetical sequence by author, here is a checklist of books covering specific areas:

General introductions: Allen, Bellamy, Bennett, Bulfinch, Campbell, Cassirer, Chadwick, Cook E, Courtney, Daniel, Eliade, Frazer, Gardner, Hartland, Henderson, Hinks, Hocart, Hooke, Kavanagh, Kellett, Kuhn, Lang, Lissner, Lump, Manuel, Olcott, Paracelsus, Porteous, Righter, Rotheim, Smart, and the encyclopedias and dictionaries.

AFRICAN MYTHOLOGY: Cardinall, Parrinder, Smith.

THE AMERICAS: Burland, Mason, Vaillant.

ANCIENT PERSIAN MYTHOLOGY: Henning, Vermaseren.

ANIMAL MYTHOLOGY: Borges and Guerrero, Clark, Freden.

ASSYRO-BABYLONIAN MYTHOLOGY: Drioton, James.

CELTIC MYTHOLOGY: Lethbridge, Sjoestedt.

CHINESE MYTHOLOGY: Werner.

EGYPTIAN MYTHOLOGY: Brophy, Cerny, Cooke, Frazer, Gray, Griffiths, James, Jayne, Murray, Plutarch, Ward.

FINNO-UGRIC MYTHOLOGY: Vorren and Manker.

GREEK MYTHOLOGY: Bailey, Bulfinch, Caillois, Campbell, Carpenter, Chadwick, Cook E, Dawson, Elderkin, Frazer, Gardner, Grant, Graves, Harris, Rotheim, Seznac, Spevack-Husmann.

INDIAN MYTHOLOGY: Archer, Ions.

JAPANESE MYTHOLOGY: Anesaki, Aston.

OCEANIC MYTHOLOGY: Beckwith, Grey, McConnel, Poignant.

PHILOSOPHY OR PSYCHOLOGY: Allen, Armstrong, Barthes, Brophy, Chaplin, Eliade, Freund, Guthrie, Hartland, Huxley, Kavanagh, Kuhn, Lindberger, Malinowski, Neumann, Reik, Zimmer.

PHOENICIAN MYTHOLOGY: Driver, Harden.

ROMAN MYTHOLOGY: Grant, Warner.

SLAVONIC MYTHOLOGY: Downing.

TEUTONIC MYTHOLOGY: Butterworth, Cook E, Ellis, Gimbutas.

Index of Gods and Men

Apart from a very few exceptions, this index contains only the proper names of gods and men; there are no topographical entries, nor are the sections in which comparative lists are given included here.

The numbers shown in italics refer to illustrations, but may also refer to textual entries on the same pages.

Acknowledgements

Photographs and illustrations were supplied or are reproduced by kind permission of the following:

Black and White
A.C.L. Brussels: 128–9, 136–7; Ateneum Museum, Helsinki: 46; Australian Information Service: 104–5, 104, 105; Barnabys: 14–15; Bodleian Library filmstrip: 16, 24, 28–9, 38, 150, 154–5, 154, 160, 161, 162–3, 172–3; Biblioteca Apostolica Vaticana: 134; Janet Bord: 33; By courtesy of the trustees of the British Museum: 38, 50, 54, 79, 80, 82, 83, 84, 85, 86, 87, 88–9, 97, 98, 99, 107, 108, 110, 114, 115, 122, 127, 154, 156, 164, 177, 180; Cliché des musées nationaux Musée du Louvre: 127; Douglas Dickins: 195; Werner Forman Archive: 52, 80, 80–1, 91, 92, 92–3, 106–7, 107, 112, 117, 174, 185, 196; Glasgow Art Gallery and Museum, Burrell Collection: 126; Michael Holford: 23, 56, 58, 59, 62, 63, 67, 72, 77, 89, 96; Alan Hutchison: 52, 53; Kunsthistorisches Museum, Vienna: 62–3, 64–5, 74–5; J. Maas and Co: 8–9; William Macquity: 47, 78, 176; Mansell Collection: 7, 19, 20–1, 22, 30–1, 30, 40, 41, 44, 45, 65, 70, 118, 124–5, 127, 140–1, 165, 168–9, 170, 178–8, 186, 187, 190, 191, 192, 200–1, 202–3; Reproduced by courtesy of the trustees of the National Gallery, London: 31–2, 57, 134–5; National Gallery of Ireland: 132; Radio Times Hulton Picture Library: 166, 167; Royal Academy, London: 40; By courtesy of Messrs Spink and Son, London: 90, 94, 95, 97, 194, 198; Statens Museum für Kunst Copenhagen: 43; Tate Gallery, London: endpapers, title page, 10–11; Theosophical Publishing House, London: 12; University of Cambridge Library: 10–11; Victoria and Albert Museum Crown Copyright: 26, 66, 68, 76–7, 90–1, 113, 123, 130–1, 138–9, 139, 143, 149, 151, 153, 157, 171, 175, 188–4; Rietbergmuseum, Zurich: 49, 55;

Colour
Bodleian Library filmstrip: 17, 145, 147, 184; Byzantine Museum, Athens: 120; Douglas Dickins: 35; Werner Forman Archive: 36, 102, 148, 181; Michael Holford: 101; William Macquitty: 35; Mansell Collection: 18; Museo del Prado/Amplicianones Mas: 147; Reproduced by courtesy of the Trustees, The National Gallery, London: cover, 182–3; The Tate Gallery, London: 144–5; Victoria and Albert Museum, Crown Copyright: 119.